Polarization is not enmity. Many will consider it as division but— in the proper context— it might be more precisely a distinction, even in extreme form. We know that these distinctions must be part of a complex system that allows new realities to emerge. Polarization— as we are experiencing it today in the USA—can (and should) be addressed constructively to avoid the breakdown of our systems. As Bernard Lonergan pointed out, we can indeed be attentive, intelligent, reasonable and responsible. We can encourage one another in the effort to understand even the worst enemy so that we can strengthen our systems and ourselves. Polarization is not a reality to which we necessarily have to succumb. We can effectively navigate and respond to it. Fr. Aaron Wessman's work reminds us, in the words of Saint Pope John XXIII, to "seek what unites, not what divides."

Dr. Andrea Bartoli
Sant'Egidio Foundation for Peace and Dialogue

We live in an age of polarization, both politically and religiously, and it is tearing our nation and our churches apart. Aaron Wessman offers a calm voice in this dangerous storm. His advice is for us to trust one another, to be more resilient and flexible, to be more curious and open-minded, to be more prudent in what we say and how we say it. He offers us personal and institutional models that might help us bridge the dangerous chasms that we have created in our world. He offers us a spirituality, rooted in Jesus and his ministry, that can help us take steps in our lives that might actually bring about reconciliation and deeper community. It is not a spirituality of cheap grace, but the costly grace of the cross that might actually lead to a new life of resurrection.

Stephen Bevans, SVD
Louis J. Luzbetak, SVD Professor of Mission
and Culture, Emeritus
Catholic Theological Union, Chicago

"What happened to my ability to listen charitably to differing opinions and thoughts? Where was kindness?" With searing humility that is surpassed only by his genuinely searching intellect, in this excellent book Fr. Aaron Wessman offers both insight and instruction. He shows people of faith how to understand, overcome, and even help heal the deep polarization that has unleashed a hurricane of destruction upon the relationships and communities of the western world, including the western Christian Church. His insights and instruction drawn from personal experience and diverse exemplars—both historical and contemporary— will inspire Christians who long to mend the social fabric that has been torn asunder.

Tod Bolsinger, Fuller Seminary, Author of
*Tempered Resilience: How Leaders are formed
in the Crucible of Change.*

Fr. Aaron Wessman's book is a *tour de force*. At a time when both Church and world are vulnerable to the most divisive of rhetorical tactics, he has uncovered a path to unity that is intellectually persuasive, spiritually penetrating, ecclesially grounded, and eminently doable. In the United States, the metaphor of fighting a culture war has left its indelible mark on the Church and the world. It will not disappear soon. Wessman aims not to dismiss the warriors on both sides or the issues for which they are waging battle but to invite them to submit to a weapons buyback in return for a spiritual discipline grounded in the witnesses of holy men and women like St. Damien of Molokai, St. Thomas Aquinas, and Dorothy Day. Is this timely? I can think of few tasks that are more urgent.

Peter Casarella
Professor of Theology and Director of the ThD
Program, Duke Divinity School

Father Robert Aaron Wessman's new text on the theme of polarization in our politics and in the Church could not be more timely. He has correctly identified polarization as a true problematic in its own right, with its own internal logic and sociological dynamic. Rather than treat the issue topically as an understandable set of responses to various "issues" he gets to the nub of the problem as a process of demonization and scapegoating that hardens ideological polarities into rigid categories that cut off further discourse. This is especially unfortunate in the Church, where charity and empathy should be evident in all of our ecclesial debates, but which has sadly degenerated of late into acrimony and hostility. However, Father Wessman is not content simply to diagnose the problem but also offers a prescriptive remedy, which is the remedy of all true reforms in the Church's history. And that is the path of sanctity, the path of the saints, and the universal call to holiness. The text is hard-hitting, but sober in tone and content, thus evincing the very civility of discourse he so rightly champions. I cannot recommend this text more highly and urge one and all to take its message to heart.

> Dr. Larry Chapp, Retired Professor of Theology,
> DeSales University; Co-Manager, Dorothy Day
> Catholic Worker Farm, Harveys Lake

This book is a much-needed Catholic response to the increasingly perilous danger of polarization in politics, society, and even the Church. For those who are unfamiliar with the dynamics of polarization, here is a well-researched and soundly-reasoned work that will get you up to speed. For those who are already well-versed, here is a vivid presentation that will provide new perspective.

For everyone, here is a bold and compelling call not to war, but into conformity with Christ's incarnational movement.

Leonard J. DeLorenzo,
Director of Undergraduate Studies, McGrath Institute
for Church Life, University of Notre Dame
Author of *Work of Love: A Theological Reconstruction
of the Communion of Saints*

In this carefully researched and deeply personal examination of the polarization in American society and Church, Aaron Wessman provides a compelling way forward for Christians to disrupt the forces threatening our destruction. Drawing from sociological, psychological, and theological resources, he describes the intensification of polarization in the twenty-first century that demonizes the "other" as the enemy and stokes rage to gain political power. He insists that Christians must replace the metaphor of war, which aids polarization, with the defining Christian metaphor of Christ's emptying in the incarnation. Wessman's prescription goes beyond a theoretical assessment, however, highlighting practical tools available to Christians to "cross over" to encounter the other and giving examples of people and organizations now putting these principles into practice. Wessman has issued a powerful call for Christians to use the spiritual resources that define us to bring healing and hope.

Douglas A. Foster
Professor of Church History, Abilene Christian
University

Jesus was not just kind. He was also *curious*. In this hopeful and inspiring book, Fr. Wessman draws a clear connection between the Christian tradition of "crossing over" to encounter the "other" and the growing movement that tradition strengthens to bridge divides in our polarized world—even and especially when it scares us.

Mónica Guzmán
Senior Fellow for Public Practice at Braver Angels
Author of *I Never Thought of It That Way: How to Have Fearlessly Curious Conversations in Dangerously Divided Times*

In this well-crafted text, Aaron Wessman showcases the damage that polarization inflicts on both society and the church. Wessman draws effectively from sociology, social psychology, and popular culture to analyze polarization, but it is the gospel that fuels the book's alternatives to separation and recrimination. The gospel's call to conversion, which transcends politics and social tribalism, is the centerpiece of Wessman's promotion of unity and reconciliation. *The Church's Mission in a Polarized World* is a vision for a future seasoned with the hope and generosity integral to authentic faith.

Richard Lennan, Professor of Systematic Theology, Boston College—School of Theology and Ministry

Jesus proclaimed that he came not to bring peace, but a sword. His earthly ministry was marked by deeply polarizing conflict between himself and the Pharisees, whom he termed "whitewashed tombs." Yet, he ate and drank with his own enemies and died for them. He loved them to the end, and he commanded us to love our enemies. In this extraordinary book Fr. Wessman asks us, in the midst of the sweeping conflicts of our time, to examine our conscience: have we become poisoned and paralyzed by hate? May we repent and learn to love!

Matthew Levering
James N. Jr. and Mary D. Perry Chair of Theology, Mundelein Seminary

It is rare in the world of theology today to find an author equally adept at both theory and practice. Fr. Wessman is just such a theologian. This book speaks eloquently the truth of our Christian faith, and to the world in which we live. It is a work of *metanoia*, conversion and so needed in our divided age.

> Fr. Denis Robinson
> President-Rector, St. Meinrad Seminary and School of Theology

Deeply knowledgeable and sincerely concerned, Fr. Aaron Wessman offers unique and thought-provoking insights on political polarization from the perspective of the pew. Wessman seamlessly weaves together academic and biblical sources to ask tough questions and demand honest answers about the Church's role in a polarized world. This book reminds us that good shepherds will rise again and shows us the path to get there.

> Joe Schuman
> Executive Director, Divided We Fall

For good reason, many people bemoan the polarization and lack of civility in American life and politics, often with a sense of despair or resignation. What can be done, anyway? Someone else should solve the problem. In this timely book, Fr. Wessman reminds us of our apostolic vocation to cross over and encounter other people, as Christ did. Faith sees with the eyes of love, and seeks the good of the other rather than their defeat. More than an inspiring call, however, Fr. Wessman explains the skills and virtues needed, and how to take those first small steps to become people of hope, courage, and hospitality.

> R. J. Snell
> Editor-in-Chief, *The Public Discourse*

The divisiveness of US politics has been the topic of countless opinion columns, but Robert Aaron Wessman expertly provides history and context to help Christians and all Americans find a way out of the storm. Both incisive and hopeful, *The Church's Mission in a Polarized World* offers practical principles from the teachings of Jesus (and examples of people who put those principles to use) to restore our civic life.

>Robert David Sullivan
>Senior Editor, *America Magazine*

This is a very significant and timely publication. It offers a detailed and sobering analysis of the emergence of polarization in both political and ecclesial life. More importantly, it offers believers a reason to hope by challenging them, and showing them how to be people "who can cross over"—to be disciples who follow the example of Jesus in seeking dialogue and true encounter with all our brothers and sisters.

>Bishop Paul D. Tighe
>Secretary (Section for Culture),
>Vatican Dicastery for Culture and Education

One of the clearest, deepest, most thoughtful and carefully researched interdisciplinary studies on polarization I have encountered. With deep respect for the power of language, Fr. Wessman's skillful use of vivid images and metaphors carry the reader into a new capacity to grapple with some of the most difficult tensions of our times. A storyteller at heart, his profound engagement with religious and cultural witnesses of dialogue, interspersed with honest and even vulnerable "show don't tell" personal examples encourage the reader to keep it real as one delves into the work needed to address divisive habits of thought and speech. This book would serve as an excellent and comprehensive text for college classes and for parish or community book clubs. His insightful interpretation of the ecclesial and cultural terrain not only generates more light than heat, but stands as a lighthouse for anyone looking for creative resources to both understand and meet this moment.

Amy Uelmen
Director for Mission and Ministry,
Georgetown Law School

Fr. Aaron Wessman has provided a much-needed exploration of how the Church can—indeed, must—respond to the toxic polarization that has strained communities, severed relationships, and derailed collaboration. He persuasively shows how a ministry of "crossing over into the storm" has a much more authentic grounding in the Gospel than the war imagery often invoked to motivate American Christians to action. This book is an important attempt to reset the conversation.

Robert K. Vischer
Interim President, University of St. Thomas,
St. Paul, MN

THE
CHURCH'S
MISSION
IN A
POLARIZED
WORLD

MAGENTA
Bold Christian voices healing divides

Living the Feminist Dream
A Faithful Vision for Women
in the Church and the World
Kate Bryan

Keep at it, Riley!
Accompanying my Father
through Death into Life
Noreen Madden McInnes

Rehumanize
A Vision to Secure Human Rights for All
Aimee Murphy

THE CHURCH'S MISSION IN A POLARIZED WORLD

Aaron Wessman

NEW CITY PRESS

Published by New City Press
202 Comforter Blvd.,
Hyde Park, NY 12538
www.newcitypress.com

The Church's Mission in a Polarized World
Aaron Wessman

3rd Printing, September 2023

Cover design and layout by Miguel Tejerina

Library of Congress Control Number: 2022951994

ISBN: 978-1-56548-549-5 (Paperback)
ISBN: 978-1-56548-550-1 (E-book)

To those who are family to me: givers of life and love, sustainers of vocation, inspiration for learning, fonts of wisdom and joy, and reasons for existence.

Contents

Series Preface

Does the book that you are about to read seem unusual? Perhaps even counterintuitive?

Good. The Magenta series wouldn't be doing its job if you felt otherwise.

On the color wheel, magenta lies directly between red and blue. Just so, books in this series do not lie at one limit or another of our hopelessly simplistic, two-dimensional, antagonistic, binary imagination. Often, in the broader culture any answer to a moral or political question gets labeled as liberal or conservative, red or blue. But the Magenta series refuses to play by these shortsighted rules. Magenta will address the complexity of the issues of our day by resisting a framework that unnecessarily pits one idea against another. Magenta refuses to be defined by anything other than a positive vision of the good.

If you understand anything about the Focolare's dialogical-and-faithful mission, it should not surprise you that this series has found a home with the Focolare's New City Press. The ideas in these books, we believe, will spark dialogues that will heal divides and build unity at the very sites of greatest fragmentation and division.

The ideas in Magenta are crucial not only for our fragmented culture, but also for the Church. Our secular idolatry— our simplistic left/right, red/blue imagination—has oozed into the Church as well, disfiguring the Body of Christ with ugly disunity. Such idolatry, it must be said, has muffled the Gospel and crippled the Church, keeping it from being salt and light in a wounded world desperate for unity.

Magenta is not naïve. We realize full well that appealing to dialogue or common ground can be dismissed as a weak-sauce, milquetoast attempt to cloud our vision of the good or reduce it to a mere least common denominator. We know that much dialogic spade work is yet to be done, but that does not keep the vision of the Magenta Series (like the color it bears) from being *bold*. There is nothing half-hearted about it. All our authors have a brilliant, attractive vision of the good.

To say that Aaron Wessman's book is a perfect fit for the series would be quite an understatement. Indeed, in many ways Magenta was created to express "The Church's Mission in a Polarized World." The term 'polarization' gets thrown around a lot, however, and one of the great features of the book you are about to read is contained in the first two chapters: a detailed, careful, precise undertaking of what it is we are attempting to resist. The rest of the book goes on to describe literally dozens of ideas and strategies for the Church to resist polarization. Of particular interest is Wessman's understanding of discipleship as "crossing over" in order to have an encounter. He does not, however, withhold clear headed warnings about the costs that come with doing so--costs which very much resemble the Focolare's understanding that authentic dialogue sometimes means connecting with "Jesus Forsaken" on the cross. Wessman's uniquely magenta vision and style of engagement perform the very thing to which he is calling us. Readers coming from multiple, plural, and even divergent perspectives will all benefit from reading this book. And may even find it to be a meeting place through which they can encounter each other.

Enjoy!

Charles C. Camosy

Series Editor

Introduction

Negative polarization and division in the United States are affecting all that we hold dear: our country, communities, schools, places of worship, relationships, and families. The scene is heartbreaking. I imagine that if you are reading this introduction, your life has been touched, in some way, by this turmoil.

Across the United States, good, thoughtful, and caring people are being subsumed into the vitriolic intensity of cultural polarization. Even as it happens, and as they try desperately to avoid it, they become something they do not want to be. They are like Dorian Gray gazing upon the monster that has materialized on the canvas even as he continues the very behavior creating the monstrosity.

Holiday family gatherings, sadly, present a glimpse of the effects of American polarization. For those who decide to gather—rather than choosing to remain at home to avoid conflict—the tension is palpable. People sit next to each other at the table in silence. Family members with shared memories—year upon year of journeying together—and who pump similar blood through their veins, have little to say. What can they talk about that will not induce rage or conflict? Religion? That is off the table. Football? Even 'America's game' is rife with pitfalls. Politics? Not a chance. Few broached subjects, especially during election cycles, are navigable. One person speaks. Another interrupts. The table is pounded. Meals end prematurely.

The microcosm of the strained family gathered around a holiday table is influenced by the macro cultural environment. Not ever, perhaps, has so much ink been spilled warning Americans of the potential for a second civil war, possible cessation, or ineluctable deepening division. Stories and articles signaling impending danger are surrounded by the very thing causing the problem: depictions of the 'other group' in a negative light, or coverage of yet another politician buttressing her popularity through negativity. The intensification of negative polarization is tearing the United States apart at the seams. Even as I write these words, I am unsure how stable the country will be when they are published.

And then there is the Church. As a Catholic priest, that the Body of Christ would be my main concern is logical. To witness members who are united in divine bonds by the power of the Holy Spirit treat their fellow Christians with contempt beyond contempt is devastating. We in the Church have consumed the same Communion, been united in the same salvific sacrifice, stood together, and witnessed our children baptized, confirmed, and married, cried on each other's shoulders at death's presence, and confessed our sins to Our Father so as to journey together to our homeland. Yet, the profound mischaracterizations and irrational hatred of our fellow brothers and sisters in Christ, sometimes simply because they share different political views or divergent ecclesial perspectives, reek of Cain's proto-rage against Abel. These behaviors and feelings belie the unity and charity Christ desired his members to instantiate in the world, and weaken the Church's evangelical mission.

Even ministers tasked with leading their flock have caved under the pressure to unite divided churchgoers. They seek wisdom from heaven about how to proceed in these unprecedented times, while knowing that they, too, contribute to a polarized milieu.

My Concern

The following book is as personal as it is communal. Even as I bemoan the carnage around me left in the wake of the cultural storm of polarization, I also realize that I am just as susceptible to its influence. I am just as concerned with what is happening inside of me.

In 2017, following nearly four years studying in Europe, I returned to America and witnessed these 'united' states breaking apart. The anger and divisiveness were tangible. They were perhaps most obvious because I had been away for so long, sheltered from the conflict and rancor.

Questions abounded. What had happened to our country? What occurred within our Church? I thought I could remain above the fray and avoid the polemics, and yet I was immediately dragged in. Why did the anger rise in me? Was I really unable to watch certain news outlets without getting upset? What had happened to some of my loved ones? Why was I so easily triggered by particular political topics or the mere mention of certain politicians? Why did my heart fill with frustration when this or that Church official spoke? What happened to my ability to listen charitably to differing opinions and thoughts? Where was kindness?

As years passed from my entrance back into the United States, social and ecclesial divisions deepened and cultural wounds festered. With urgency, I began searching for answers.

Though much remains unknown, as the cultural markers of polarization continue to shift and evolve, this book is an attempt to synthesize some of my research into this field. If you feel the same urgency as I do, or if you are simply a fellow pilgrim along this road, I hope the following words are, in some way, like Virgil's guidance leading the way out of the underworld.

A Way Forward

Though it pains me to have to make this admission, I believe that part of the way forward can only be found in admitting that the Church in the United States has, in part, lost her way through this valley of tears. I will, with trepidation, suggest some of the ways that this has likely taken place. However, I suspect that the lasting influence of this book will not arise from my critique. The lasting influence will come by the way in which readers, myself included, ponder within themselves to what extent negative polarization has touched their own lives. Only in recognizing where each of us needs to grow will the path forward be seen more clearly.

And yet there is always hope. God provides the Church a way forward during every age she encounters. Our age is no different.

Though I am certainly not claiming any kind of prophetic insight, I will argue in this book that part of this way forward can be found in reflecting upon, and imitating, Jesus' incarnational movement. Through his *kenosis*—in emptying himself and 'taking on flesh'—the Son of God crossed over into a world filled with strife, division, and destitution, to encounter and to save that world. He did not spurn or hide from the world. Mysteriously, he embraced it in every way but sin. His followers, not being divine, can only analogously—and prudently—imitate this movement. Nevertheless, I contend that it is within this incarnational movement—a crossing over to the 'other' with Christ—that the Church can recover the correct path to her journey home. Only in doing so will the Church sufficiently differentiate herself from and purify polarizing impulses, thereby bringing salvation and unity to a world in need of both.

Structure

To explore the aforementioned themes, chapters one and two of this book will utilize political, sociological, psychological and theological research to answer the question: What is polarization? These chapters will pull from wonderfully written work addressing the sociopolitical reality of polarization in the United States. I will argue that polarization is best understood as the formation of two storms swirling and causing havoc in these fractured states of America.

Chapter three will pivot to an investigation of polarization and the Church. This chapter will proceed as a kind of examination of conscience for the Church—for Christians (including myself)—to ask how the logic of polarization is possibly affecting our discipleship as Christians, and undermining the fundamental tasks of the Church in the world. Rather than explore individual theological challenges and disagreements existing within the Church, this chapter will investigate how polarizing tendencies seem to be limiting the Church's ability to live fully the mystery she is to be in and for the world.

Chapter four will specifically analyze one of the problematic responses the Church has taken to counter the effects of polarization. The 'culture war' metaphor will be diagnosed as a cancer within the Church's missionary endeavors. Jesus' incarnational movement will be proposed as the medicinal metaphor that can potentially bring healing.

Chapters five and six will unpack the consequences of the metaphor of Jesus' incarnational movement for the life of the Church. What it means for the Church to 'cross over' to embrace the other, and to bring about 'salvific encounters' in the world, will be explored. In delving into the nature of Jesus' incarnational movement, and what this metaphor means for the Church in a polarized world, hopefully, I will begin to chart a path forward that can be pursued prudently in these tumultuous times.

The final chapter will explore contemporary examples of people who, and organizations that, are participating in aspects of Jesus' 'incarnational movement' in this world. These examples provide hope in the midst of the storms, and can serve as inspiration for Christians (and others) going forward.

The Scope of this Project

I love the United States, even as I recognize its complex and imperfect history. Traveling around the world has deepened my appreciation of this vast and beautiful country that I call home. Nevertheless, my primary concern in this book is not how polarization is affecting America in general. Many people have sought to address this theme. They have presented possible ways forward from a societal and political perspective. Their thoughts will infuse these pages. However, this book is neither about political policy, nor individual political parties or candidates.

What I am vitally concerned about are my primary loves: Christ and the Church he has founded. I write this not to signal that these loves are in any way lived perfectly in my life, but because I will be providing a critique of something I—and I know others—hold dear. I desire to show how polarization is affecting, or has the potential to affect, the Church, and how the Church might respond in light of her call to live as Jesus' followers in this world. Through every generation, the Church has encountered various challenges that shape her missionary vision and practice. Polarization is our challenge. This does not mean, of course, that the words within this book are divorced from broader societal and political problems in the United States. The Church does not exist in a vacuum. Quite the contrary, the more the Church lives according to her nature, the more the cultures and societies in which she is present, and which influence her, benefit from her presence, and she from them.

There is little doubt that the Church will respond to the challenge of polarization. In many ways this is already happening. What that response should or could be is at stake. Hopefully, the following pages provide some assistance to readers and stimulate courage, so that Christians can see the age in which we live more clearly and respond with grace to follow more fully the call God has spoken.

Chapter One

What is Polarization? Sorting, Homogenization, and Intensification

The Perfect Storm

I have always been fascinated with storms. Growing up in Minnesota, I remember observing dark, ominous clouds gather over rolling cornfields, viewing weather maps on television predicting snowfall accumulation, or occasionally hiding in our basement from the threat of tornadoes. Fascination turned to fear, however, when later in life I was assigned as a priest to a Catholic mission in eastern North Carolina and encountered my first hurricane.

It was 2018, and I, along with the other residents of the southeastern United States, watched the tempest that would be named Florence form off the coast of Africa. As the saying goes, the elements were right for a perfect storm: amassing warm moisture rising and swirling around a central point; low wind shear, unable to disrupt the clustering of clouds around the eye of the storm; and heat bringing greater intensity as the temperatures rose.

This quite large and remarkably slow-moving system advanced toward us. As I scrambled to execute my emergency plan, I could not help but wish I were back in

Minnesota. No midwestern weather event compared to this terrifying behemoth approaching my home.

In many ways, hurricanes and societal polarization have a lot in common. Rather than moisture-filled clouds surrounding the eye of the storm, human beings are sorting themselves by clustering together in groups around political, geographical, or ideological poles. Rather than low wind shear ensuring uniform strength and movement within the hurricane, there is minimal human diversity—by way of, for example, ideas, life-visions, values, or theology—interacting with clustered groups ensuring increased group homogenization. And rather than heat strengthening storms, triggered emotions or fragile identities can intensify both group belonging and negativity felt by members within groups, as well as aversion to and fear of others outside the group.

A difference, of course, within this metaphor, is that a hurricane usually exists alone and in an isolated region. Polarized groups, however, function like multiple hurricanes interacting with each other, causing, at times, seemingly irreparable relational and cultural damage from coast to coast.

Journalist and political commentator Ezra Klein has produced a helpful volume (one which I will refer to often throughout this book) summarizing an abundance of research on polarization. In *Why We're Polarized*, he alludes to these three contours, *sorting*, *homogenization*, and *intensification*, as he seeks to describe the contemporary polarized milieu.[1] He writes: "When I say the political

---

1. Ezra Klein, *Why We're Polarized* (New York: Avid Reader Press, 2020). There are many causes and contours of polarization. These three provide a framework to address many other details regarding this cultural phenomenon. For a comprehensive list of nearly 50 causes and contours, see Peter T. Coleman, *The Way Out: How to Overcome*

[and other cultural] coalitions are becoming more sorted and more polarized, I mean only that: there is less ideological overlap [increased sorting and homogenization], fewer of us are caught in the middle [increased sorting and homogenization], and there is more tension between the poles [intensification]."[2] Existing alone, or even in pairs, these contours do not suffice to produce polarization—at least not the toxic type that exists in the United States. Together, however, they create the perfect cultural storm.

The remainder of this chapter will look at the first two of these contours of polarization: *sorting* and *homogenization*. A brief interlude will serve to introduce the theme of *intensification*, and this will be taken up in more detail in the following chapter.

Sorting

To say that people in the United States are sorting themselves means that they are increasingly choosing, directly or indirectly (i.e., flowing from indirect consequences of their actions) to cluster around, or exclusively associate with, other like-minded people.

Sorting is quite normal, and occurs in many forms. Christians, for instance, group together to worship with other Christians, especially of their own tradition. Republicans come together with other Republicans to fundraise or protest, and Democrats do the same. Soccer players need other players to compete; musicians

---

Toxic Polarization (New York: Columbia University Press, 2021), 26. For another accessible book on these themes, see Nolan McCarty, *Polarization: What Everyone Needs to Know* (Oxford: Oxford University Press, 2019).

2. Klein, *Why We're Polarized*, 35.

require others to form a band. Technology entrepreneurs often move to demographic bubbles to increase creative exchange with like-minded people. Catholic intellectuals, administrators, and students cluster together to participate in the mission of a Catholic university.

People naturally cluster around like-minded people and form groups. Indeed, joining a group with whose members one has little in common, or when one has little-to-no-interest in the purpose of the group, is exceptional, and goes somewhat against the human desire to belong and the human attraction to what is familiar. Sorting alone, therefore, is not overly problematic. But it is one element creating the perfect storm of polarization, and so deserves some attention.

Not all of the ways that people sort themselves will be covered in this chapter. However, because of the significant role they play in moving a society toward polarization, three forms of sorting are worth further investigation: geographical, identity-based (e.g., political, racial, religious, psychological, or cultural), and virtual (the forms of online media with which people interact).

Geographical Sorting

Journalist Bill Bishop has famously documented geographical sorting in his book *The Big Sort: Why the Clustering of Like-Minded America Is Tearing Us Apart*. Within a very mobile country like the United States, many people can make decisions about where to live. Over the last few decades, these decisions have become, as Bishop documents, anything but random. Human beings have sorted geographically, choosing to live around others within particular regions, cities, or towns who, for instance, think like them, look like them, worship like them, have the same interests as them, and enjoy the same kinds of entertainment. As Bishop states:

> When [people] look for a place to live, they run through a checklist of amenities: Is there the right kind of church nearby? The right kind of coffee shop? How close is the neighborhood to the center of the city? What are the rents? Is the place safe? When people move, they also make choices about who their neighbors will be and who will share their new lives. Those are now political decisions, and they are having a profound effect on the nation's public life.[3]

Geographical sorting in the United States exists in such a pronounced way that, today, it is possible to refer to a rural and urban divide,[4] a coastal and heartland divide, a geographical divide correlated to wealth,[5] and even a geographical divide based on identity.[6] This latter type of geographical sorting based on identity preferences has become so formative in American society that it requires a closer look.

Identity-Based Sorting: Politics

Throughout this book, I will regularly be referring to the concept of 'identity.' Though this is a complex theme, what

---

3. Bill Bishop, *The Big Sort: Why the Clustering of Like-Minded America is Tearing Us Apart* (Boston: Mariner Books, 2009), 5–6.

4. David French, *Divided We Fall: America's Secession Threat and How to Restore Our Nation* (New York: St. Martin's Press, 2020), 31–39. Klein, *Why We're Polarized*, 39.

5. Amy Chua, *Political Tribes: Group Instinct and the Fate of Nations* (New York: Penguin Books, 2018), 137–164.

6. Klein, *Why We're Polarized*, 38.

is being referred to here, in part, are the various ways in which each individual answers the question: Who am I?[7]

Some of the aspects of one's identity, that is, how one comes to answer this question, come through personal choice, preference, or reflection. Other aspects come from family, friends, genes, or inheritance; others, from a combination of influences. How an individual integrates her identity is a lifelong process, and will include both implicit (that is, minimally developed or integrated aspects of who one is) and explicit (resulting from personal reflection and ownership) elements.[8]

So, for instance, a young woman might identify as a person who is a Democrat who practices Buddhist meditation (these are personal choices which are, in part, influenced by family, friends, and education), who comes from a Mexican immigrant background (this is partially a family inheritance and also a source of personal pride), who sees herself as successful because of landing a good-paying job which rewarded her for her educational achievement (this was encouraged by her family and resulted from personal effort guided by mentors), and who is Catholic 'enough' to go to Mass with her extended family during holiday visits (this was informed by family tradition and taken as a personal choice). These various ways of providing meaning in her

---

7. For more on the theme of identity, see Robert Aaron Wessman, "The Options for Identity-Discernment in a Secular Age," *Church Life Journal*, December 5, 2017, https://churchlifejournal.nd.edu/articles/what-are-the-options-for-authentic-identity-discernment-in-a-secular-age/.

8. On the notion of integrating one's identity, see E.F. Schumacher, *A Guide for the Perplexed* (New York: Harper, 2015), 26–38. See, also, Robert Aaron Wessman, "Kenotic Solidarity in a Splinterizing World: A Balthasarian Response to the Polarization of Contemporary Society," in *Answerable for Our Beliefs: Reflections on Theology and Contemporary Culture Offered to Terrence Merrigan*, ed. Peter De Mey, et al. (Leuven: Peeters, 2022), 679–697.

life all form her identity, likely are felt more personally than mere intellectual ideas (though they are related to these), and are some of the most important facets of who she is.[9]

Particularly important to the identity of many people are, among other aspects, the religious tradition they are a part of, especially if they regularly practice this way of life, the racial or ethnic groups with which they identify, and the political parties to which they belong. It is to the last of these that I now turn—people's political preferences—looking specifically at how this identity type has sorted geographically throughout the United States.

Most of us probably have the experience of watching a news outlet as vote counts emerge following regional or national elections. One thing that stands out, as overzealous analysts manipulate massive smart screens displaying maps of the United States, is that red states and blue states exist—there are regions of the United States that are strongly for Democrats and others thoroughly aligned with Republicans.

What might be surprising is that this has not always been the case. Historically, there was much more political diversity evenly distributed throughout the United States. As Klein comments on this reality, "for much of the twentieth century, the idea of red states and blue states wouldn't have made much sense."[10] What is telling is that now there are not just red and blue states, but red and blue *counties*, many of which have little chance of changing color. These are known as 'landslide counties.'[11]

---

9. On this point, see Klein, *Why We're Polarized*, 60–79.
10. *Why We're Polarized*, 38.
11. The notion of 'landslide counties' can be found in the research of Dave Wasserman. I came across the research through French and Klein. See Klein, *Why We're Polarized*, 39. Klein also documents the

Political commentator and former attorney David French, in his work reflecting on polarization in the United States, writes on the increasing number of 'landslide counties' throughout the country. As he states:

> Most Americans live in a state that's either solidly Republican or solidly Democrat, and it's not just the states that are unified around a single political party. Consider the growth of the so-called landslide county, a county that one party or the other wins by at least twenty points. In 1992 only 38 percent of American voters lived in a landslide county. In 2016 that number hit a record 60 percent.[12]

In other words, according to the data, regional sorting by way of people clustering together in particular counties has occurred so thoroughly that 60 percent of Americans live in a county where there is virtually no chance for an opposing political party to win an election.

Of course, the existence of these counties affects the political landscape of the country, potentially determining how parties make decisions about campaigning or spending money, or how party leaders listen to the needs of, or understand and empathize with, the people in various areas. If there is no chance for a politician to win in a particular county or state, a politician simply is not going to listen much to those people's needs—she likely won't even visit the area. The existence of landslide counties also affects whether or not people from a particular, oftentimes massive, region feel represented and understood by a party, especially if that party holds important politi-

---

existence of 'extreme landslide counties.' These counties have quintupled in the United States in the last 25 years.

12. French, *Divided We Fall*, 32.

cal positions or influence. When a Democrat is President of the United States, for instance, people in vast regions of rural America likely will feel quite underrepresented. Perhaps more importantly, however, for the purpose of this book, the demographic makeup of landslide counties tends to suggest that most people throughout the United States are unlikely, within the county they live in, to have any in person, sustained interaction with people from a different political persuasion. Consequences from this reality abound.

One repercussion is that people are unlikely to have meaningful conversations with members of another political party that could deepen thought or challenge assumptions through the exchange of hopes, values, stories, or dreams. They are also less likely to collaborate in efforts that could lead to a feeling that they share a mutual home, such as, supporting the same little league baseball team, hosting fundraisers together when a person has an unexpected sickness or problem in the family, worshipping or praying together in the same church, or working together to improve a neighborhood. Many of the ways in which people grow to appreciate each other, and experience in each other the dignity that each person shares in being human, even if they share different political views, will not likely occur. And if these interactions do not take place in person, the view that a person has of an opposing political party and its members will likely be informed through media representations, which often tend to distort reality and paint a negative picture of the other (more on this later).[13]

---

13. Jaron Lanier, *Ten Arguments for Deleting Your Social Media Accounts Right Now* (New York: Henry Holt and Company, 2018).

Identity Based Sorting: Race, Religion, and More

The existence of red states (majority Republican) and blue states (majority Democrat), and red counties and blue counties, necessarily implies other important types of sorting based on identity because of the way in which political parties have sorted around other identity markers. In other words, statistically, being a member of a certain political party correlates with other markers of identity, be they racial, psychological, or theological, for example. This is not to say that there are not exceptions to these categorizations within political parties. But the trends are demonstrated in the data.[14] I am not going to burden readers with all the statistics, but only summarize some of the many ways markers of identities are sorted geographically and politically throughout the United States.

For instance, blue regions will likely have more religiously 'unaffiliated' people, along with people who do not attend church regularly, whereas red regions will likely have more Christians, especially evangelicals, and more people who indicate that they attend church regularly.[15] Blue regions will contain more people who do not think you need to believe in God to be a moral person, whereas in red regions a rising number of people believe the opposite.[16]

As the United States becomes more racially diverse, blue regions are more likely to reflect that diversity, while red regions will be representative of a whiter population. Blue and red regions are also differentiated 'psychologically,'

---

14. See Lilliana Mason, *Uncivil Agreement: How Politics Became Our Identity* (Chicago: The University of Chicago Press, 2018), 24–44; French, *Divided We Fall*, 31–39; Chua, *Political Tribes*, 156–158; Klein, *Why We're Polarized*, 36–48.
15. See French, *Divided We Fall*, 31–39.
16. Klein, *Why We're Polarized*, 38.

where, among other ways, the former will likely contain more people who are 'open' to diverse experiences, while the latter will have more people concerned with 'tradition' and 'order,' and who are somewhat skeptical of change.[17]

Finally, among many other statistics that mark stark contrasts between blue and red states, people in these regions partake in different forms of entertainment.[18] Though 'entertainment' is not likely as intimate an identity marker as race or religion, it does determine what people have in common. Following similar patterns of sorting, people in blue regions are more likely to watch *Game of Thrones* or the NBA, and those in red regions are more likely to watch NASCAR, WWE, or *The Walking Dead*.

I want to pause and note a few points about the significance of geographical sorting based on identity and politics.

First, it has not always been the case that political parties sorted around many of the identity markers mentioned above. The novelty of this type of sorting emerged as certain preferences were sorted among political parties (on account of historical processes that will not be investigated here[19]), and those parties and preferences sorted geographically. Commenting on this novelty, Klein states that people of differing political parties once "looked alike, lived similar lives, and thought only somewhat differently," but now they belong to "two warring camps that look different, live different lives in different places, and find themselves in ever-deeper disagreement."[20] That this

---

17. Klein, Why We're Polarized, 43–48.
18. See Klein, Why We're Polarized, 41–42; French, Divided We Fall, 36–39; Chua, Political Tribes, 156–158.
19. See Klein, Why We're Polarized, 1–48. See, also, Mason, Uncivil Agreement, 24–77.
20. Klein, Why We're Polarized, 36.

type of sorting is novel suggests that the United States is dealing with somewhat unprecedented challenges in the history of the country.

Second, as groups split politically and this split aligns with other types of identities, there becomes less incentive to reach across and pursue common ground. Political scientist Lilliana Mason, who has conducted extensive research on polarization, including that found in her book *Uncivil Agreement*, summarizes this well, and it is worth quoting in its entirety:

> [Democrats and Republicans] have little reason to find common ground. They have become increasingly homogeneous parties, with Democrats now firmly aligned with identities such as liberal, secular, urban, low-income, Hispanic, and black. Republicans are now solidly conservative, middle class or wealthy, rural, churchgoing, and white. These identities are increasingly aligned so that few identities affiliated with either party are also associated with the other side. White, religious, and conservative people have little incentive to reach across to the nonwhite, secular, and liberal people in the other party. What superordinate goals do they have? In which places do they mix with opposing partisans? Few of today's salient social groups help either party to reach across the divide.[21]

Third, even if people become motivated to cross over the divide, a further challenge arises. It is important to note how grand the canyon between these geographic regions can be, and how difficult it can be to cross that divide to relate to, or enter into dialogue with, the other side, when

---

21. Mason, *Uncivil Agreement*, 26.

the differences held by people living in these areas are based on identity markers. Watching *Game of Thrones* or being more 'open' to change, in comparison with watching *The Walking Dead* and being somewhat more skeptical about change, are not differences that directly affect matters of life and death, nor are they issues that are likely to elicit a strong response, if challenged. They are important. But few people are willing to debate intensely the merits of psychological preferences or sacrifice their life for a fictional series.

A person's feelings or thoughts regarding race, politics, *and especially religion*, however, are different. These are extremely sensitive and formative, and do have an influence on matters of life and death—including, from a theological standpoint, issues related to eternity, heaven and hell. Political decisions made about healthcare or immigration *can* affect whether people live. Moreover, the extent to which a person extends human dignity to all people, from the unborn to those on death row, matters for sustaining biological life, and for consideration regarding eternal life (based on one's theological position). People are much more willing to protest on behalf of these positions, debate them vigorously, and hold strong emotions about them. In one real sense, people in red and blue regions will hold starkly different opinions regarding *the most important aspects of life*. When whole sections of the United States share little in common in reference to these matters, the chasm between people inhabiting these regions can seem to grow exponentially, and appear to be even more difficult to traverse, even if one has some motivation to attempt it.[22]

---

22. On this point, see French, *Divided We Fall*, 34–37.

One might hope that even though the United States has sorted geographically, people might encounter differing opinions, and come to see the inherent worth of their political opponents or people of different religions, for instance, through the sites they visit online, the types of media they watch, or the groups or friends they follow on social media. However, this kind of exposure to other groups, along with cultivating a greater empathy toward those who are different yet endowed with inherent dignity, are not likely to happen online.

Online Sorting

Research regarding online activity, especially the use of social media and its effects on human beings, is still being produced and interpreted.[23] In reference to the topic of 'sorting,' however, there is evidence that life online will reflect, in many ways, life offline, with a few distinctions.

To begin, it is helpful to think about online activity as being somewhat of an extension of offline activity. At least initially,[24] when people first use social media and begin engaging in online activity, they are most likely to 'friend' folks they already know or with whom they have at least some tangential connections. It is typical, moreover,

23. On this point, see Lanier, *Ten Arguments*. See, also, Nancy Jo Sales, *American Girls: Social Media and the Secret Lives of Teenagers* (New York: Vintage Books, 2017). See, also, Paul Barrett, et al., "How Tech Platforms Fuel U.S. Political Polarization and What Government Can Do About It," September 27, 2021, https://www.brookings.edu/blog/techtank/2021/09/27/how-tech-platforms-fuel-u-s-political-polarization-and-what-government-can-do-about-it/. See, also, Chris Bail, *Breaking the Social Media Prism: How to Make Our Platforms Less Polarizing* (Princeton: Princeton University Press, 2021).

24. See Bail, *Breaking the Social Media*, 26–27. See, also, Lanier, *Ten Arguments*, 80–81.

for many social media users to follow groups or institutions they are already interested in or search for familiar topics online. A California vegan who practices mindfulness and does not believe in God is not likely to 'friend' a pastor of an evangelical church, follow a local NRA group in West Virginia on Twitter, research the latest happenings concerning characters from *Duck Dynasty*, or search for conservative theological discussion groups through Google. People's online behavior is going to follow some similar patterns to their behaviors offline.

There are also indications that certain features of online reality reinforce (i.e., promote) sorting, and even deepen polarization by heightening the intensification of negative feelings toward other groups. For instance, the algorithms used by social media companies tend, on the one hand, to present information to users that matches their predetermined preferences and interests, or that reflects previous online activity and choices.[25] If people tend to spend time watching, or responding to, videos of Republican members of Congress, for instance, or if they react on Facebook to conservative posts, they are likely to be fed more of the same while online, resulting in the perpetuation of America's sorted groups.

On the other hand, if there is a discrepancy between online and offline behavior, it is often that online behavior, driven by algorithms, typically intensifies polarizing tendencies, and deepens sorting, rather than doing the opposite.[26] The intensification of negative online behav-

25. Will Oremus, et al., "How Facebook Shapes Your Feed," October 26, 2021, https://www.washingtonpost.com/technology/interactive/2021/how-facebook-algorithm-works/.

26. See Barrett, "How Tech Platforms." Barrett notes that: "Our central conclusion, based on review of more than 50 social science studies and interviews with more than 40 academics, policy experts, activ-

ior occurs because the algorithms used by social media companies favor negative posts that stimulate negative feelings. These negative feelings are often directed toward members of another group. As these negative feelings amplify, people tend to grow more committed to their chosen groups, and more averse to anything remotely related to an opposing group (more on this topic in chapter two).

Furthermore, if people search out certain media sites explicitly, or come across news stories on social media or other formats, they are not likely to be exposed to meaningful presentations of people from different political parties. Nor will they likely view stories that challenge many of their assumptions about life, or that invite them to form a more nuanced vision of reality—including a nuanced vision of an opposing political group. It is almost common knowledge that different news outlets cater to different sorted groups.[27] People recognize that this or that news outlet is either 'left' or 'right' leaning. This implicit assumption is backed by research that shows that media business models have increasingly shifted over the last half-century to cater increasingly to viewers' desires.[28] And what viewers desire are stories and coverage that reinforce an insider-outsider group mentality. In other words, media outlets provide viewers with content that concretizes their sorted group preferences: The stories many networks cover often deepen people's appreciation of their own in-group by presenting these groups in an uncritical, positive light,

---

ists, and current and former industry people, is that platforms like Facebook, YouTube, and Twitter likely are not the root causes of political polarization, but they do exacerbate it."

27. See Lanier, *Ten Arguments*, 57–66.
28. Klein, *Why We're Polarized*, 139–158; see, also, Mason, *Uncivil Agreement*, 42–43.

while stimulating aversion toward, and even fear concerning, opposing groups, by presenting them negatively.[29]

To be sure, however, there are exceptions to some of the patterns named above, specifically, that online activity always matches offline activity.[30] For instance, many people send the infamous email bomb they wish they could un-send, share uncharacteristic Facebook posts or videos they hurriedly delete before they are seen or shared by too many, create the occasional pseudo-identity on social media, or are exposed to certain behaviors, ideas, or images online they would not likely have encountered, at least not in the same way, offline.[31] Some research does suggest that online activity, for some people, tends toward producing more intense or extreme behavior, wherein people who otherwise appear 'normal' in person become 'trolls' online.[32] Others, who would normally provide a 'moderating' voice in political discussions, are discouraged from sharing any political views online for fear of the repercussions related to doing so.[33]

Nevertheless, even though people's digital identities and activities do not always match perfectly with offline identities and activities, there does not seem to exist strong evidence that current online activity would circumvent sorting. The opposite seems likely to be the case. If Americans have sorted into identity groups

29. Lanier, *Ten Arguments*, 77–85. Bail, *Breaking the Social Media*, 10; 38; 41–53.
30. Bail, *Breaking the Social Media*, 68–81; 105. Though online and offline personalities do not always match perfectly, Bail's research does not suggest that online activity will circumvent 'sorting.'
31. See Sales, *American Girls*.
32. Bail, *Breaking the Social Media*, 38; 54–67.
33. Bail, *Breaking the Social Media*, 107.

offline, that sorting is only likely to be maintained, and perhaps deepened, online.

Homogenization

Now that I have presented some of the relevant research regarding the first contributing factor to America's cultural storm, *sorting*, I am going to shift to the subject of *homogenization*.

Returning to the original metaphor of this chapter, that of the hurricane, homogenization within a hurricane exists because there is not enough wind shear to significantly influence the increasingly uniform formation of the storm's swirling, moisture-filled clouds. If low wind shear exists, it either has negligible influence on the hurricane, due to the ferocity and power of the unidirectional movement within the storm, or the wind is subsumed into the storm altogether, and bends to the direction and movement of the storm, thereby disappearing.

Homogenization, in reference to polarization, refers to the way in which clustered or sorted groups increasingly become more uniform. Increasing uniformity can exist, for instance, when members of a group become more ideologically similar, thinking the same way with the same kinds of ideas (even biases and prejudices), or where people within a group increasingly share similar cultural interests, purposes in life, or values. In essence, as will be explored in more detail below, homogenization occurs because diversity around or within sorted groups is too minimal and has little effect on the group; or, the types of diversity within or around a group disappear by succumbing to the pressures of the group. The following are several ways in which these trends exist.

Uniformity through Sorting

Group uniformity flows somewhat naturally from sorting, and examples of how sorting tends to produce homogenization have already been alluded to above. When people cluster together around a particular purpose, end, idea, or preference, there is going to be certain homogeneity or uniformity already present in the group.[34] In one sense, it is possible to say that there is a predetermined bias of the group around which the members cluster.[35] For instance, if people come together to form a soccer club, those with strong desires to play baseball, football, or basketball are not likely to be as many in number as those who want to play soccer. If a member of the group has some interest in football, it is likely placed aside under pressure from the group's overall desire to play soccer.

I have already documented research that explores many of the ways in which geographical or online sorting produce regions or groups of increasing homogeneity in the United States, from pockets of the country which have become more thoroughly Democrat or Republican, to other regions that have become more racially uniform, or to the existence of online groups that are virtually sorted into particular preferences. What is remarkable is that even after being sorted homogenously, groups, by the very dynamic of human behavior within groups, tend toward eliminating diversity and bringing about uniformity. This phenomenon deserves a closer look.

---

34. Mason, *Uncivil Agreement*, 41.
35. See Cass R. Sunstein, "The Law of Group Polarization," *John M. Olin Program in Law and Economics Working Paper*, no. 91 (1999), online at https://chicagounbound.uchicago.edu/law_and_economics/542/. See, also, French, *Divided We Fall*, 63–70.

Homogeneity by Group Pressure

Group dynamics and the psychology of groups, and how both of these affect polarization, will be explored more thoroughly in chapter two when the topic of *intensification* is addressed. However, it is important to note, in reference to the theme of *homogenization*, the way in which group dynamics tend toward bringing about uniformity. This is especially important to consider as sorted groups, which already have an inherent bias within the group, continue to form and develop in the United States.

Various types of research exist which suggest that when a group forms for a particular reason, around, for instance, a cause, idea, or preference, and when diversity of thought or perspective within that group consists only within a small minority, increasing uniformity within the group is likely to occur.[36] In other words, by their very nature, groups tend to bring about homogenization.

One study[37] that suggests how people can succumb to group pressure to go along with a preference of the group was constructed by showing different individuals a card with a single line on it. Along with this single-lined card, they were shown a card that had three lines on it, of three different lengths, where one of the lines was quite clearly of the same length as the single line from the initial card. The people were asked to choose which line of the arranged three matched the length of the original single

---

36. On this point, see Klein, *Why We're Polarized*, 81–98. See, also, French, *Divided We Fall*, 63–67. See Chua, *Political Tribes*, 100–106.

37. This is a well-documented study by Solomon E. Asch, a professor at Swarthmore College. See Solomon Asch, "Opinions and Social Pressure," *Scientific American* 193, no. 1 (1955): 1–7, online at https://www.lucs.lu.se/wp-content/uploads/2015/02/Asch-1955-Opinions-and-Social-Pressure.pdf.

line. Without group pressure, i.e., when they were able to make this decision alone, individuals matched the lines *incorrectly* less than one percent of the time. Not bad.

When asked to accomplish the same task, now within the context of a group, and after witnessing other people in that group who, for the sake of the experiment, matched the single line with one of the three that clearly did not match, the number of *incorrect* responses by individuals rose to over 36 percent. In other words, in a simple task of matching lines that were obviously matches or not, group pressure significantly influenced people to defy the conclusion of their own senses, and choose based on the decision of the group. Group pressure was so influential, that people were over 36 times more likely to make an incorrect choice than when they were deciding alone.

This is one case among many that shows how strong an influence group pressure can have on individuals, tending to reinforce uniformity within a group. Clearly, when the uniformity brought about has to do with choosing lines, the consequences are not grave. However, it is easy to imagine how group pressure can influence people to think or do any number of things they normally would not do without the pressure of the group.

David French, in reflecting on the strong tendency in human beings to cave to the pressure of group dynamics, summarizes this concept well:

> At some point in our lives virtually every one of us has gone along with the crowd when the opinions of the crowd matter to us and when we perceive risk in defying its judgment. At worst, we enthusiastically participate. Sometimes our silence constitutes in

effect consent. It's hard to be our best selves and risk shame in the peer groups that matter most.[38]

As I will explore in chapter two, the pressure to conform to a group becomes even more problematic when what the group tends to be pushing is a kind of animus toward the other, or even a hatred or denigration of other people, simply because they are not part of a particular group to which one belongs.

Uniformity by Decision

Sorting and group dynamics tend, in many cases, to bring about group homogenization inadvertently. In other words, in some cases, homogenization is not necessarily specifically sought out. There are ways, however, within American political, religious, and social culture that uniformity has been specifically pursued by members of a group through intentional decisions and actions.

Political parties, for instance, have increasingly promoted party uniformity for the sake of purported political expediency.[39] Over a half-century ago, political parties in the United States had far greater diversity of thought and preference within the various parties. There existed conservative Democrats and liberal Republicans, for example, and any number of preferences and perspectives within both parties, particularly on the local level. Because of party diversity, split-ticket voting was common.

Those who ran the political parties of the time, however, saw this diversity within the parties as a weakness in the political process. Their solution was to push for

---

38. French, *Divided We Fall*, 67.
39. On this point, see Klein, *Why We're Polarized*, 1–17.

uniformity, especially around policy issues.[40] As the years progressed, two very distinct parties emerged, giving voters clear, obvious choices with little ambiguity in the middle. In other words, partisan distinction did not occur by chance, but was intentionally and systematically sought out by party leaders.

Mason, writing on this reality, notes that parties not only wanted ideological homogeneity, they also wanted to send 'cues' to voters that they either did or did not belong to a political party. This reinforced group uniformity, attracting certain types of people and dissuading others. Put differently, political parties catered, and promoted themselves, to different sociocultural groups in the United States, in the hope of making people's choice to belong to a particular party easier to determine. As Mason states:

> Due to the clearer distinction between the parties, Americans had far more simple cues to follow. These cues helped citizens to understand that a highly religious Christian who is also wealthy and white will feel most at home among Republicans. Similarly, a secular, less-wealthy, black person will feel more comfortable surrounding herself with Democrats. The parties, by providing increasingly clear cues, have helped Americans to know which party is their own.[41]

Advertising these cues was successful, and the parties split based, in part, on the ways in which leaders sought to cater to particular groups.

---

40. I do not focus extensively in this book on policy issues. However, for a helpful analysis of the polarization of policy issues, see Pew Research Center, "Political Polarization in the American Public," *Pew Research Center*, June 2014, https://www.pewresearch.org/politics/2014/06/12/political-polarization-in-the-american-public/.

41. Mason, *Uncivil Agreement*, 42.

Yet another push for uniformity over the last few decades has existed within religious groups. Bill Bishop documents this movement within some Christian churches, for instance. According to his research, churches determined it was 'evangelically' expedient for them to grow their churches by pushing for greater uniformity within the churches. As he states:

> The strategy [by the churches] was as simple as like attracts like. The new and crowded megachurches were built on the most fundamental of human needs: finding safety within the tribe. The method worked so well that now these techniques for creating group cohesion through like-mindedness are employed in most churches.[42]

The result, Bishop concludes, from the process of homogenization within churches, is that "American churches today are more culturally and politically segregated than our neighborhoods."[43]

Promoting uniformity or homogeneity for the sake of some predetermined value or reason has not existed solely in the political or religious realm. As research shows, homogeneity has also been sought out in the United States in various other ways, such as economically, where businesses lump groups of people together to cater to different subgroup preferences,[44] and culturally (e.g., as in 'nature conscious' or 'cultural creatives' groups), where communities are formed and developed specifically around certain kinds of lifestyles or thematic ways of living.[45] In other

---

42. Bishop, *The Big Sort*, 159.
43. Bishop, *The Big Sort*, 159.
44. Bishop, *The Big Sort*, 257.
45. Bishop, *The Big Sort*, 212–217.

words, across a broad spectrum of social and cultural situations, uniformity is pursued as a preference.

Interlude

So far in this chapter, I have provided an overview of two of the elements, which are contributing to bringing about the hurricane season of polarization in the United States. Whole sections of the country are sorting geographically, and this is happening around some of the most important facets of people's lives: religion, politics, race, economics, and more. Not only are Americans sorting; there are also processes in place that, within those sorted regions and groups there is an increasing movement toward uniformity and homogenization. The result is that large sections of the United States have little in common with other sections, the commonalities that perhaps do exist are slowly fading away, and there is little incentive and opportunity to associate with groups that are different.[46]

With sorting and homogenization alone, it is possible to interpret the present cultural situation as being somewhat innocuous: like-minded people are getting together for the sake of preferences and desires, becoming more homogeneous as they come together, and perhaps finding it less possible for them to understand, relate to, or talk to people who are different than them. What makes sorting and homogenization most problematic in the American context is that both are joined with *intensification*. People not only do not associate or have little reason to associate with those of another group; they increasingly hold

---

46. This is one of the main arguments of Amy Chua in her book *Political Tribes: Group Instinct and the Fate of Nations*. I will explore this idea further throughout this book. See, also, Mason, *Uncivil Agreement*, 26.

on to their perspectives and positions within their group in ways that can cloud their judgment or even influence them to act in contrarian, somewhat vicious ways, while they simultaneously grow in their aversion for, and even in some cases hatred of, the other. This is the subject of the next chapter.

Chapter Two

What is Polarization? Intensification

"Things are Heating Up"

About a week before Hurricane Florence reached the eastern shores of the United States, I was standing on those very shores with my feet digging into the sand, the breeze blowing lightly across my face, and the inimitable ocean fragrance filling my lungs. I had decided to take a short retreat to a cottage outside of Emerald Isle. And a retreat it was. At that moment, I had the beach all to myself, as most people were already evacuating. I would soon follow, returning to my home farther inland to prepare for the storm.

Wanting to relish the moment a little longer, I walked to the waterline, and waded in. The chilly sensation woke up my skin and was a reminder that summer had come to pass. What proved to be a moment of tranquility for me, standing small in front of the horizon's expanse, starkly contrasted the violence and destruction from the storm that would soon occupy the shores upon which I was standing.

The irony, of course, is that the water that felt cold to me on the shores of North Carolina has actually been getting incrementally warmer, according to statistical data.[1] Ocean waters throughout the world, in many places, are following suit. These incremental increases in temperature occurring over decades, though difficult for human beings to detect by simple touch, seem to be adding to the intensity of some hurricanes and increasing the destruction caused around their paths.[2]

In a similar way, the hurricanes of polarization, the polarized groups people belong to, are intensifying. As people have sorted into groups and regions throughout America, and as these groups increasingly become more uniform (chapter one), there is an intensification of the way in which these groups exist within society. This is witnessed, on the one hand, in how polarized groups are becoming more important and influential in people's lives. Like swelling hurricanes exerting influence on wind, clouds, and most everything in their path, so starkly opposing political groups are increasingly influencing American culture in general, and individuals' thoughts and actions in particular. Intensification is evidenced, on the other hand, by how people within their sorted, segregated groups are increasingly engaging members of other groups in hostile and bitter ways. Like massive hurricanes colliding in a sci-

---

1. See, for instance, Rebecca Lindsey and Luann Dahlman, "Climate Change: Ocean Heat Content," *Climate.gov: Science and Information for a Climate-Smart Nation*, August 17, 2020, https://www.climate.gov/news-features/understanding-climate/climate-change-ocean-heat-content.

2. See Alan Buis, "How Climate Change May Be Impacting Storms Over Earth's Tropical Oceans," NASA: *Global Climate Change*, March 10, 2020, https://climate.nasa.gov/ask-nasa-climate/2956/how-climate-change-may-be-impacting-storms-over-earths-tropical-oceans/.

fi nightmare, the cultural destruction left from vitriolic, polarized groups clashing is immense and all too real.

This present chapter will provide an investigation of both sources of intensification: the augmented importance of political-cultural groups, and the increasing negative engagement between these groups. This analysis, when coupled with the previous chapter's description of *sorting* and *homogenization*, completes an overview of the three elements bringing about the multi-hurricane storm of polarization.

The (Increasing) Importance of Group Belonging

To understand why polarized groups in American society are so important and influential, and increasing in their level of importance for many people, it is necessary to begin by investigating the role that groups play in the lives of human beings in general. Only in understanding the immense importance of group belonging to people's lives will the significance of belonging to political (and other) groups be sufficiently appreciated. I will begin this analysis by looking at psychological perspectives on groups and group belonging and follow this by theological and sociological inquiries into the same theme.

Group Belonging as Necessary for Survival: Psychological Perspectives

One of the underlying premises in social and evolutionary psychology is that human beings are essentially social creatures who rely upon groups for meaning, identity, security, and survival. This premise is linked to the way that human beings, as a species, evolved within groups.[3] Social psychologist Kipling Williams, along with his colleagues, emphasize this point:

> We are essentially social creatures. Throughout most of our evolutionary history, we lived, loved, and labored within the confines of small, intimate groups where we knew, and were known by, each member. Within these groups, we were sheltered from the elements, protected from predators, and ultimately given the opportunity to propagate and prosper.[4]

To be part of a group meant life. To be separated from a group, or to have one's group weakened in any way, could mean death. This was a lived truth for early human beings.

Because of the importance of group membership for survival, human beings developed certain biological mechanisms within them, often triggered in the brain, to 'remind' them of the necessity of group belonging. In other words, human beings evolved with 'switches' in the brain. If one's membership in a group is threatened, these switches turn on, affecting various aspects of a person's emotional and physical constitution, sometimes in negative ways, warning them that they need to respond by monitoring and countering the threat.[5] The existence of these reactions to group exclusion has been researched and documented by psychologists.

---

3. For a further investigation into this theme, see Jonathan Haidt, *The Righteous Mind: Why Good People are Divided by Politics and Religion* (New York: Vintage, 2013).

4. Kipling D. Williams, et al., ed., *The Social Outcast: Ostracism, Social Exclusion, Rejection, and Bullying* (New York: Psychology Press, 2005), 1–2.

5. Jaap W. Ouwerkerk, et al., "Avoiding the Social Death Penalty: Ostracism and Cooperation in Social Dilemmas," in *The Social Outcast*, ed. Kipling Williams, et al. (New York: Psychology Press, 2005), 321–327.

Research suggests that if people perceive their membership in a group is threatened, they go through physiological responses similar to those caused from physical harm and bodily stress.[6] The effects of this 'social pain' are posited to be worse for human beings physically than those caused by smoking or diabetes.[7] Furthermore, feelings of loneliness, which are often linked to group exclusion, can negatively affect cognition. The pain caused from exclusion seems to limit people's ability to think clearly, such that, when lonely, people are more likely to make decisions that go against their own needs and health.[8] Loneliness can also negatively affect sleep, where people who describe themselves as lonely unknowingly wake more often during the night. Waking is likely a kind of survival response arising from the perception of being separated from a group.[9] Finally, among other evidence of the importance of groups for human beings, research suggests that complete loss of group belonging is linked to mental illness and overall diminished functioning within day-to-day life.[10]

Being separated from a group may not negatively affect people today in the same way as it did their ancestors. However, group belonging is still vitally important,

6. Geoff MacDonald, et al., "Adding Insult to Injury: Social Pain Theory and Response to Social Exclusion," in *The Social Outcast*, ed. Kipling D. Williams, et al. (New York: Psychology Press, 2005), 77–90.

7. Wendi L. Gardner, et al., "Social Snacking and Shielding," in *The Social Outcast*, ed. Kipling D. Williams, et al. (New York: Psychology Press, 2005), 229.

8. See John T. Cacioppo and Louise C. Hawkley, "People Thinking About People," in *The Social Outcast*, ed. Kipling D. Williams, et al. (New York: Psychology Press, 2005), 91–108.

9. Klein, *Why We're Polarized*, 58.

10. Kipling D. Williams and Lisa Zadro, "Ostracism: The Indiscriminate Early Detection System," in *The Social Outcast*, ed. Kipling Williams, et al. (New York: Psychology Press, 2005), 22.

and the psychological research above highlights this fact. What is more, researchers have found evidence of various ways human beings will adjust their behavior to remain part of a group or will act in certain ways to preserve the groups to which they belong. These tendencies are both conscious and unconscious human responses, once again signaling the importance of groups.

The mere threat of exclusion from a group can initiate an almost unconscious process within a person whereby the excluded member begins to assess the situation, determine the reasons for exclusion, and search for ways to 'replenish' one's connectedness and belonging to a group.[11] This process typically does not cease until a kind of stasis is reached, and the group member perceives that his membership is secure. Moreover, some research suggests that people who feel rejected will increase their conformity to a group. One way this is done is by mimicking people within the group in ways that are thought to bring about rapport with group members.[12] Interestingly, this tendency toward mimicry is also somewhat unconscious, being triggered within a person because of the perceived threat of exclusion.[13] Finally, in other research, instances have been documented wherein, after a group perceives a threat to its existence, individual members will diminish 'self-serving' behaviors, and increase their cooperation among group members in order to preserve the group.[14]

---

11. Cynthia L. Pickett and Wendi L. Gardner, "The Social Monitoring System: Enhanced Sensitivity to Social Cues as an Adaptive Response to Social Exclusion," in *The Social Outcast*, ed. Kipling Williams, et al. (New York: Psychology Press, 2005), 213–226.

12. Ouwerkerk, "Avoiding the Social," 321–327.

13. Jessica L. Lakin and Tanya L. Chartrand, "Exclusion and Nonconscious Behavioral Mimicry," in *The Social Outcast*, ed. Kipling Williams, et al. (New York: Psychology Press, 2005), 279–288.

14. See Haidt, *The Righteous Mind*, 219–284.

Psychologically, groups are extremely important. They serve primal desires for protection, safety, and survival. Threatened group membership can be terrible for human beings. Before providing a more thorough analysis below, it is possible to speculate how this relates to the contemporary polarized situation in the United States.

People are likely to be emotionally, psychologically, and physiologically connected to their political-cultural groups in profound ways that go beyond their own intellectually discerned preference for the group—these connections will be, in some ways, evolutionary. If these groups are threatened, or if a person feels they are losing membership in these groups, negative consequences occurring at the psychological and biological level may be felt—consequences that can be worse than those suffered from smoking or diabetes! In response to these negative consequences, people will likely seek to preserve their political-cultural groups due to, in part, a primal urge to survive.[15]

Before looking specifically at the role political groups play in people's lives, and how some of the psychological trends documented above are manifest within political groups, I want to look at the importance of groups through the theme of 'fragility.' Groups are not just extremely beneficial from a psychological perspective. They can help alleviate human fragility, and this can be understood both theologically and sociologically.

Fragility and the Need for Group Belonging

If the global pandemic that began in early 2020 taught people anything, it is that human existence is fragile. Not

---

15. See Lakin, "Exclusion," 280.

in over a century had the world been reminded, on such a universal scale, of how vulnerable people are to a hidden, microscopic danger.[16] This fragility was amplified when, rather than being a moment for unity, the pandemic became a divisive experience, especially politically, and showed the limits of some human institutions to provide leadership and guidance during times of crisis.

Of course, there are many types of fragility, from the vulnerability of homelessness, the liminality of migrancy, the frustration of inadequate employment, the experiences of types of bigotry and racial or sexual hatred, the uncertainty induced on account of major demographic shifts, particularly those currently occurring in the United States, or the struggle felt from wrestling with the multitudinous effects of poverty.[17] Fragility, then, exists when those elements essential for the fullness of life are not met.

One source of fragility, which is relevant to the role played by political and other cultural groups in people's lives, is that associated with either not knowing, or not being secure in, one's identity. Related to meaning, belonging, and purpose, this type of fragility goes to the very heart of a person and is judged by some to be nearly as important to survival as food, water, clothing, or shelter.[18] Evidence suggests that this kind of fragility is both operative within human beings and amplified by cultural factors in the United States.[19]

---

16. See, for instance, John M. Barry, *The Great Influenza: The Story of the Deadliest Pandemic in History* (New York: Penguin, 2018).
17. On the theme of 'fragility,' see Chua, *Political Tribes*, especially 137–196.
18. See, for instance, Viktor Frankl, *Man's Search for Meaning* (Boston: Beacon Press, 2006). See, also, Williams, *The Social Outcast*.
19. For an analysis regarding this type of fragility, see Sebastian Junger, *Tribe: On Homecoming and Belonging* (New York: Twelve, 2016).

Original Fragility and the
Need for Group Belonging

The Judeo-Christian tradition, in its foundational story concerning human existence found in the book of *Genesis*, speaks of the fragility of being human, of not knowing one's identity, and connects this fragility to a loss of communal or group belonging.

As the book of *Genesis* indicates, God has established human beings within creation that is best described as paradise. Adam and Eve live together in concord, they are in a harmonious relationship with God, and they are 'embedded'[20] in creation (cf. Gn. 2:1-25). Within this original framework, human beings know who they are—their lives are purposeful and meaningful. They are children of God, above all else, and have been created to love God. They are part of a larger 'family' or 'group,' united to each other in bonds of mutuality and complementarity. Indeed, the interrelated identity of man and woman is characterized in Eve coming from Adam's side (Gn. 2:21-22), and in Adam only finding his perfect partner in Eve (Gn. 2:20b). Human beings understand their role within creation and live a peaceful existence within the overall web of life. Because of all this, their identities are secure (Gn. 2:25).

Of course, as the story goes, humans choose to sin (Gn. 3:1-7), and this disrupts original communion and group belonging, and the meaning gained from this belonging.

As a result, after the Fall, human beings hide from God, indicating that they have forgotten their fundamental relationship with God, their creator (Gn. 3:8). Where they once walked with God in the garden, they now flee from

---

20. On the notion of 'embeddedness,' see Charles Taylor, *A Secular Age* (Harvard: Belknap, 2007).

God, and misunderstand God (Gn. 3:10). They become estranged from each other as man and woman, indicating a loss of interpersonal identity, an undermining of their group belonging (Gn. 3:16). They begin to experience a type of shame, which suggests not being completely at home within their social environment (Gn. 3:7). When invited to speak truthfully about their situation, they prevaricate, showing their lack of knowledge about who they are and how they are to act (Gn. 3:12-13). Ultimately, human beings are exiled from paradise (Gn. 3:21-24).

The creation story is replete with wisdom, and one does not have to espouse the Judeo-Christian tradition to appreciate the truth found in this narrative. To be human after the Fall is, in part, to struggle to feel at home, whether bodily, relationally, or with one's purpose in life. It is, in some ways, to long for that home—that community— that always seems somewhat unattainable. Being human means, at times, loneliness, while paradoxically not being completely comfortable when around others. To be human is to grope for meaning, while not being certain when it is found.[21] After the exile from Eden, people struggle to answer the foundational question regarding identity: Who am I?

To be sure, the biblical narrative provides a witness of hope. But this hope only comes through humanity being reconstituted back within a community, and finding relative security in their identity. God's action after Adam and Eve's ostracization from Eden is one of gathering humanity back together into a new group, raising up a new community, a chosen people and, ultimately, establishing a new people through Jesus Christ in, and through, the Church.

---

21. On this point, from a scientific perspective, see Bill Bryson, *A Short History of Nearly Everything* (New York: Broadway Books, 2003).

This movement to restore human beings to their place within the world, to remind them of their identity, *and to do so within a group*, however, cannot be understood without recognizing first the fragile experience of being human.

The Judeo-Christian tradition provides more than a hint of the importance of groups for human beings. Human beings were created to be embedded in groups of meaning and identity. This embeddedness is normative, and it is the default position in which people are most likely to feel at home. Once lost, it can only be restored through the groups to which people belong. The group of highest importance for Christians is, of course, the Church. And the Church, being the Body of Christ, is no ordinary group. Yet this does not discount the possibility that the desire for all group belonging is, in some ways, a response seeking, often frantically, to restore what has been lost. Groups can alleviate some of the negative experience of original fragility, healing the loss of identity felt deep within the human heart.

Of course, not all people subscribe to the Judeo-Christian narrative. What is notable, however, is that sociological research adds to this analysis by telling a story of a similar kind of fragility—connected to the loss of belonging and identity—and a related need for group belonging.

Social Fragility and the Importance of Groups

In his work titled *Liquid Modernity*, sociologist and philosopher Zygmunt Bauman (1925–2017) provides a sociological analysis of Western culture. For Bauman, over the last number of centuries, there exists an increasing cultural trend, influenced by human behaviors, toward the 'melting away,' or liquidation, of societal structures and social groups that provide identity, meaning, belonging, purpose, and security to people.[22] As these social structures (groups) melt away, human beings find themselves existing somewhat individualistically as they face the experience of fragility. As Bauman's analysis highlights the increasing importance of groups in contemporary society, it deserves a closer look.

Imagine, for instance, it is 500 years ago, and a person is standing on a giant ice cube.[23] The ice cube represents her identity, that is, how she makes sense of her life: who she is, what is of value to her, and what her purpose is for living. Contributing to the ice cube is her family, providing her a role within the family, values, and a trade to which she will almost certainly contribute in some capacity. The cube also is shaped by the land and geography around which she lives, whose contours influence her vision of the world. Included, as well, are the town she lives in, along with her neighbors, from whom she is likely to 'receive' a spouse. This geography is also a place apart from which she is unlikely ever to live. The intermingled politics and religion shared by those living together, moreover, solidify the cube by providing meaning, morality, and rituals, which bind and unite people, and secure a sense of social and moral solidarity.

Historically, within Western society, given the ways people organized their lives, the ice cube upon which the woman from this example stands would have been nearly frozen solid.[24] It rarely would show signs of melting. Even

---

22. See Zygmunt Bauman, *Liquid Modernity* (Cambridge: Polity, 2012), especially viii–ix.

23. The cover art for Bauman's 2012 edition of *Liquid Modernity* depicts a melting ice cube.

24. See Bauman, *Liquid Modernity*; see, also, Taylor, *A Secular Age*; see, also, Francis Fukuyama, *Identity: The Demand for Dignity and the Politics of Resentment* (New York: Farrar, Straus and Giroux, 2018).

with some intentional effort, it would have been difficult to reshape or chip away that upon which she stands. At almost no moment during her life in this era would she ask the question: Who am I?[25] Her identity would have been secure.

In modern times, however, according to Bauman, within the cultures in which most people live in the Western world, including the United States, on account of a multiplicity of different changes that took place within society, the ice cube is all but melted away, leaving many people fragile, feeling as if they are 'drowning,' struggling to find meaning, unsure of their purpose, and forced to navigate the important questions of life—of identity—somewhat on their own.[26]

How, exactly, does the present cultural situation arise? To be sure, Bauman provides a lengthy analysis. For the purpose of this section, a few details will suffice.

For instance,[27] people move, and they are uprooted from the familiarity of home, geography, land, and the people of their town. They seek to recreate community and meaning in a new place, and find this difficult, because so many others are transient. Soon, they become frustrated in these attempts. Families are less stable, extended families are far-removed, separation and divorce occur, values are not as easily passed down generationally, and people are left trying to understand who they are in light of these changes. Technologies evolve, jobs leave, and people move again, trying to find employment. Even political structures are liquefied; revolutions come, democracy is established,

---

25. See Fukuyama, Identity, 64–65.
26. Bauman, Liquid Modernity, 21.
27. For Bauman's narrative, see Liquid Modernity.

and then questioned, and then hangs on precariously.[28] And the overall sacred canopy cracks, shatters and, in some cases, disappears; people cease practicing religion, or religion becomes almost solely a personal matter, formed from the multiplicity of options available, and sometimes disconnected from its original purpose of binding people together.[29] One's identity, rather than being a solid, frozen cube on which to stand, nearly melts away.

Whereas in past societies people 'received' their identity in life, and this was supported by societal and communal structures, the modern person is tasked with creating meaning, belonging, and their identity in the world, a process Bauman calls individualization.[30] Referring back to the previous metaphor, people are tasked with pushing and pulling together amorphous and slippery liquid, attempting to solidify it, no matter how difficult. As Bauman states: "Keeping fluids in shape requires a lot of attention, constant vigilance and perpetual effort – and even then the success of the effort is anything but a foregone conclusion."[31]

Those who have the skills, personality and requisite resources generally welcome the process of individualization. They utilize the treasured, and rare, social capital at their disposal. Educational resources further help them navigate a fluid and changing world, and a more stable family life usually assists them in managing 'liquid modernity' more successfully. For others, particularly for the underclasses of society, they nearly fail to meet the

---

28. See Steven Levitsky and Daniel Ziblatt, *How Democracies Die* (New York: Broadway Books, 2019).
29. For more on this point, see Robert Aaron Wessman, "The Church's Witness in a Secular Age: A Hauerwasian Response to Privatized Religion," *Missiology: An International Review* 45, no. 1 (2017): 56–66.
30. See Bauman, *Liquid Modernity*, 30–31.
31. See *Liquid Modernity*, 8.

demands. Overwhelmed, they try to find their place in the world. They are fragile within the liquidation of meaning, struggling to form their identity in life, and sometimes forced to do so alone.[32]

This might seem like a bleak analysis of Western culture, especially when considering the perspective of the underclasses. But Bauman is not alone in noting these cultural trends. For instance, professor of international relations and political scientist Francis Fukuyama, writing on the theme of identity, agrees with much of Bauman's description.[33] Fukuyama highlights, moreover, that in responding to an individualized cultural experience, many people choose to reconstitute their identity through group belonging, *often out of desperation*. He states:

> Human beings are intensely social creatures whose emotional inclinations drive them to want to conform to the norms surrounding them. When a stable, shared moral horizon disappears...the vast majority of people do not rejoice at their newfound freedom of choice. Rather, they feel an intense insecurity and alienation because they do know who their true self is. The crisis of identity leads...to the search for a common identity that will rebind the individual to a social group and reestablish a clear moral horizon.[34]

In other words, a paradox seems to exist in contemporary culture. Modern culture tends toward undermining group belonging, as well as the identity and meaning one receives from within a group, even as human beings react against this tendency—this fragility—sometimes out of despera-

---

32. Bauman, *Liquid Modernity*, viii.
33. Fukuyama, *Identity*, 35; 61–73.
34. Fukuyama, *Identity*, 56.

tion, by seeking to form and join groups, and to regain a sense of belonging, as well as the meaning and purpose that flow from belonging.[35]

To be sure, not all people feel fragility at the same level of intensity on account of living in liquid modern culture. Some people will likely enjoy the individuality from this milieu. They will appreciate the freedom afforded by a culture that allows them to create meaning, identity, and purpose, somewhat on their own, without the overarching pressures of traditions, families, or solid social structures. Or they will enjoy a culture that allows them, in some cases, to leave behind unhealthy groups or identities, and to reestablish others that promote their well-being. Others will simply not feel the urgency for social inclusion in order to find security, purpose and meaning in life.

However, the sociological research suggesting the challenges arising from liquid modern culture is substantial and is supported by numerous case studies looking at specific demographics within society, especially in America.[36] When this research is seen in light of the theological and psychological research presented above, a pattern emerges. Groups are vitally, and increasingly, important to

---

35. Compare, for instance, the research of Robert Bellah and Robert Putnam, with that of Amy Chua. Bellah and Putnam argue that aspects of modern society leave people isolated, struggling to form community; Chua argues that modern society is extremely tribal. I tend to think both perspectives are correct. The narrative above highlights how this can be the case. See Robert N. Bellah, et al., *Habits of the Heart: Individualism and Commitment in American Life* (Berkeley: University of California Press, 2008). See Robert Putnam, *Bowling Alone: The Collapse and Revival of American Community* (New York: Simon and Schuster, 2020).

36. See Nancy Isenberg, *White Trash: The 400-Year Untold History of Class in America* (New York: Viking, 2016); Charles Murray, *Coming Apart: The State of White America, 1960–2010* (New York: Crown Forum, 2021). See, also, Mason, *Uncivil Agreement*, 41–42.

human beings, specifically in how they help people overcome fragility, and provide meaning, identity, security, and a necessary sense of belonging. When these groups are threatened, or belonging is compromised, as is often the case in contemporary culture, fragility is enhanced. Interestingly, Bauman and Fukuyama suggest that one of the groups that come to play an important, and sometimes exaggerated role, in people's lives is the political group to which they belong.[37] These groups are the subject of the next section.

The Increasing Importance of Political Groups

Now that I have presented research regarding the importance of groups and group belonging for human beings, I want to examine the increasingly significant role political groups play in people's lives in the United States. To begin, I will investigate an idea flowing from political science research that suggests that political identities have become 'mega-identities.' I will then look at some data that indicates the growing influence political groups have on people's lives.

Political Identities as Mega-Identities

Historically, in the United States, the political group a person belonged to was one group among many, and the other groups they belonged to were not necessarily linked to their political group.[38] Part of their identity, furthermore,

---

37. See Bauman, Liquid Modernity, 37–38; 168–201. See, also, Fukuyama, Identity, 59–73.
38. See Mason, Uncivil Agreement, especially at 1–4;14; 60.

came from their political group, but they understood themselves in a diversity of other ways, and these facets did not necessarily relate to their political identity. Fifty years ago, for instance, being from rural America, having a large family, practicing the Christian faith, and being white did not necessarily mean that a person identified as Republican. Neither did coming from the city, self-identifying as an atheist, or having no children necessarily imply one was a Democrat. Today, however, statistically speaking, this is not the case.[39] What has changed in the contemporary situation is that one's political identity is increasingly *the* identity with which most of a person's identities align: it is a mega-identity.[40]

Lilliana Mason, in her aforementioned research found in *Uncivil Agreement*, utilizes the term mega-identity in a paragraph that brings together much of the research presented thus far in this book, touching on the themes of sorting, homogenization, and group dynamics. She states:

> The American political parties are growing socially polarized. Religion and race, as well as class, geography, and culture, are dividing the parties in such a way that the effect of party identity is magnified. The competition is no longer between only Democrats and Republicans. A single vote can now indicate a person's partisan preference as well as his or her religion, race, ethnicity, gender, neighborhood, and favorite grocery store. This is no longer a single social identity. Partisanship can now be thought of as a

---

39. See Mason, *Uncivil Agreement*. See, also, Bishop, *The Big Sort*.
40. This concept is discussed by Mason, Klein, and French in their research.

mega-identity, with all the psychological and behavioral magnifications that implies.[41]

What Mason is suggesting, is that historically non-political identity markers are now increasingly difficult to distinguish from one's political identity. And the identity markers that align with one party do not present themselves in a significant way in the other party. A person may not immediately connect shopping at a particular grocery store, moving to a particular area of the United States, engaging in a certain hobby, or practicing a particular religion with politics, but the reality is that these identities and practices often align quite perfectly within a political group. The result is that both political groups in the United States have become like large hurricanes, with fierce political winds forming and influencing all or most aspects of people's lives, with all the most important identities and aspirations of a person being pulled into the storm, and consequently swirling around within it under the pressure of politics. Put another way: one's political identity becomes their identity (a mega-identity), and one's political group (a mega-group) is nearly indistinguishable from the other groups to which a person belongs.

Examples signaling the truth of mega-identities exist all around, and one place this can be seen is driving down the interstate in the United States.[42] In the slow lane, for instance, one sees a thin, healthy-looking twenty-something driving a tiny, environmentally friendly Toyota Prius, detailed with a "Feel the Bern" bumper sticker, a Black Lives Matter decal, a Darwin Fish magnet, a Pride Flag hanging from the mirror, and Trader Joe's reusable grocery bags

---

41. Mason, *Uncivil Agreement*, 14.
42. For more on 'mega-identities,' see Klein, *Why We're Polarized*, 68–75. See, also, Chua, *Political Tribes*, 137-196.

lying on the back seat. In the fast lane is a white, portly man driving a loud, black smoke emitting dual exhaust four-by-four raised pickup truck flying Trump and American flags, with a shotgun mounted in the cab, stainless steel male organs hanging from the hitch, a Jesus Fish on the bumper, and a decal of a cartoon character urinating on a Nike symbol on the back window. These are both examples of mega-identities on wheels. They are symbolic of the coalescing of two people's various identity markers into distinct, politically saturated and influenced identities.

Some Consequences of Mega-Identities

In reflecting on the theme of mega-identities, Ezra Klein argues that one of the consequences stemming from this reality is that political participation is no longer solely about strictly political considerations or outcomes, such as working for and supporting a particular political candidate, or winning an election for a particular party. On account of the reality of mega-identities, political participation and outcomes relate to, and affect all (or at least most of), the identities in a person's life.[43]

For example, flowing from some of the analysis in chapter one, since the Republican Party today aligns most closely with practicing Christians, who espouse that you need to believe in God to be a good person, who live more often in rural areas, and who are more likely to be white, a win for the Republican Party can seem like a win for Christians, white people, or for those who are intimately attached to rural America. It might even be perceived as a win for God! Likewise, political activity can be viewed

---

43. See Klein, *Why We're Polarized*, 68–74.

as more than supporting a party. Working on behalf of a political party can seem like working to shore up all the most important facets of a person's life: from their most cherished values, or their sexual or religious identity.

Inversely, negative consequences in the political realm are about much more than politics. Losing an election, for instance, is not solely about one's party losing, it is about one's identity 'losing.' It is the very meaning, purpose, and cherished values of one's life being threatened— and having this occur in an already fragile world. For some Christians, for example, an election loss might be interpreted as undermining God's own kingdom, as so-called 'atheistic liberals' gain political power and implement their ideology. For an LGBT person, an election loss might seem to threaten one's family, or denigrate the treasured way in which one seeks to love in life. Negative election consequences, for members of both parties, can seem to endanger the very mega-group to which one belongs. And this group, for many people, plays *the role* of providing a vital source of survival and protection in a fragile world.

Moreover, if an aspersion is cast against a party or a party's candidate, it can easily be interpreted, or at least felt, as an aspersion cast against one's faith, God, race, family, or sexual identity. When feelings around one aspect of a person's identity are triggered, feelings around other identity markers can easily be triggered as well, with an intensification of feelings of fear, harm, or insecurity, especially on account of the factors related to the psychology of group belonging, as previously investigated. A kind of downward spiral can exist, increasing the negative harm perceived and felt.[44] It is possible to imagine people

---

44. Klein speaks of a logic of polarization. See Klein, *Why We're Polarized*, xix. See, also, Greg Lukianoff and Jonathan Haidt, *The Coddling*

thinking: "That politician is attacking not only my political candidate, but everything I hold dear in life!"

Another way that the reality of mega-identities amplifies the importance of political parties is that very few areas of life are now left untouched by politics. For example, since Republican identity is most often aligned with Christian identity, there is political incentive for a politician to appeal to this identity.[45] In appealing to this identity, it automatically becomes politicized. Political leaders can be perceived as spokespeople of Christianity or the Church and can even influence the way Christians understand or live out their faith. Political leaders might not have the expertise, or the legitimate authority, to speak on behalf of Christianity. However, politicians can easily be perceived as leaders of the mega-group, which happens to encompass Christian identity.

Political influence is growing in other areas beyond Christianity as well. For instance, political leaders tell people how they should respond to a sport, such as football, how they should dress, what businesses they should patronize, or how they should entertain themselves.[46] All of this points to why a Nike commercial featuring Colin Kaepernick can elicit such strong responses within people, or why a person would choose to eat or not to eat at a Chick-Fil-A restaurant. These realities have become political realities and are entangled with all the emotions related to group belonging, fragility, and the ups and downs of election cycles. Especially if a person is affected by negative feelings regard-

---

of the American Mind: How Good Intentions and Bad Ideas are Setting Up a Generation for Failure (New York: Penguin Books, 2018), especially at 125–141.

45. Andy Stanley, Not in It to Win It: Why Choosing Sides Sidelines the Church (Grand Rapids: Zondervan Reflective, 2022).

46. Klein, Why We're Polarized, 69–71.

ing an opposing party, or facing an unfortunate political loss, a simple shoe commercial can elicit those feelings, and then touch on any number of the other identities a person espouses. There is a kind of 'political creep,' in which every area of life is, or has the potential to be, politicized.

Among other ramifications of the reality of mega-identities is that when most of a person's identities converge and align within one party, there are fewer bridges existing between political identity groups. With fewer bridges, people have fewer reasons to cross over to relate to out-group members. In fact, research suggests that the more one's identities align with one's political party, that is, the more solidified one's mega-identity is, the less likely one is to socialize with, or tolerate, a member of the out-group.[47]

Klein summarizes this well: "When we share identities with each other, they can act as a bridge. You're a '90s kid and I'm a '90s kid, so let's talk about how the '90s were the best decade for music. But when our identities separate us from each other, they can be a moat, widening the distance between us."[48] With little in common with the other political mega-identity group, few natural bridges remain. And this means that the political group a person belongs to will likely be the sole voice influencing their lives on political (and other) matters.

The Rising Influence of Party Identity

The existence of mega-identities suggests that political groups have a growing influence over people's lives. Much

---

47. Mason, Uncivil Agreement, 61–77, especially at 70.
48. Klein, Why We're Polarized, 71.

data exists demonstrating this influence, some of which will be presented here.

Reflecting some of the psychological research presented above concerning group dynamics, one way that party identity influences people is that it motivates those who belong to a party to 'mimic' the identities or characteristics defining that particular party, while downplaying other out-group identity markers.[49] Across a wide range of identity markers, including race, sexual orientation, religion, and class, people attempt to blend into their political groups by 'shifting' their identities. Commenting on this reality, David French states:

> There are some Latino Republicans who functionally shed their Latino identity. There are gay Republicans who shed their LGBT identity. There are religious Democrats who shed their faith and white Democrats who strain to find a non-white ethnic identity.[50]

Of course, the ability to shift one's identity to match the perceived identity of an in-group political party is much more likely in an environment where political groups have sorted and become homogenous, and identities are not shared across various groups. In other words, the existence of mega-identities facilitates identity shifting, because people can more-easily determine which identity markers they need to embrace and which to downplay.[51]

Party identity also biases how people think about, and act toward, others, particularly those within their own

---

49. See French, *Divided We Fall*, 81–83. French is utilizing the research of Patrick Egan found in "Identity As Dependent Variable: How Americans Shift Their Identities to Align with Their Politics," *American Journal of Political Science* 64, no. 3 (2020): 699–716.

50. French, *Divided We Fall*, 82.

51. French, *Divided We Fall*, 83.

political group. This research is, once again, reminiscent of what was presented above regarding group dynamics. FFor instance, a study conducted by political scientists Sean Westwood and Shanto Iyengar,[52] noted that people, when determining who to grant an imaginary scholarship to, were more likely, after reviewing applications, to reward supposed members of their own party a scholarship rather than out-party members. Party identity, in this experiment, was more influential on decision making than race or academic achievement.

In an unrelated study, people were presented an imaginary policy initiative and asked to express their favorability toward it. Participants were more likely to favor a policy proposal if it appeared to be affiliated with their own party.[53] What is more (and perhaps counterintuitive), even when the content of a policy contradicted their predetermined ideas regarding how society should respond to meet various challenges (i.e., the actual policies participants would normally support), they favored that which was related to their political party rather than content that matched their policy preferences. In other words, party identity trumped policy preferences, even for those significantly engaged in the formation of political policy.[54]

Yet another trend that has emerged over the last few decades is the increasing way in which party affiliation has become one of the main factors influencing people in

---

52. Shanto Iyengar and Sean J. Westwood, "Fear and Loathing across Party Lines: New Evidence for Group Polarization," *American Journal of Political Science* 59, no. 3 (2015): 690–707. See, also, Klein, *Why We're Polarized*, 75–79.

53. See Klein, *Why We're Polarized*, 86–89.

54. Evidence of other forms of political bias can be found in Bishop, *The Big Sort*, 300–301.

regard to political activity.[55] Patrick R. Miller and Pamela Johnston Conover, in a paper titled "Red and Blue States of Mind," documented this reality.[56] When looking at many different factors that can increase a person's likelihood to feel amplified feelings of fury or competition during an election, from one's policy preferences, education level, church attendance, race, and others, strong party identification was the most determinative cause. Put differently, the stronger one's party identity was, the more likely one was going to be enraged during an election. Similarly, strong party identification was also the factor that was most likely to motivate people to get involved politically, again, surpassing many other factors, such as policy preferences, class, or race. What influenced people to cast a vote or work on behalf of a candidate was strong party identity.

The only variable that seemed to influence people to be more actively engaged in political matters than the strength of their own party identity was the negative feelings they had toward the out-group political party. As Miller and Johnston Conover state: "So, when partisans endure meetings, plant yard signs, write checks, and spend endless hours volunteering, what is likely foremost in their minds is that they are furious with the opposing party and want intensely to avoid losing to it—not a specific issue agenda. They are fired up team members on a mission to defeat the other team."[57] For those actively involved in politics, anger and competition motivate, increasing the likelihood of negative polarization. It is to this latter theme that I now turn.

---

55. See Klein, Why We're Polarized, 61–64.
56. See Patrick R. Miller and Pamela Johnston Conover, "Red and Blue States of Mind: Partisan Hostility and Voting in the United States," Political Research Quarterly 68, no. 2 (2015): 225–239.
57. See Klein, Why We're Polarized, 62. This quote is taken from Miller and Conover, "Red and Blue," 234.

Increasingly Hostile Engagement Between Political Groups

In this chapter, I have shown how important group belonging is in general for human beings, and how this importance manifests itself in the political-cultural groups to which people belong. Now I will investigate what it means for political (and other cultural) groups to increasingly relate to each other in hostile and negative ways. To appreciate this reality, it is necessary to return to one final point about group dynamics: how human beings are wired for inter-group conflict.

Wired for Inter-Group Conflict

In the late 1960s, social psychologist Henri Tajfel (1919–1982) set out to investigate inter-group behavior.[58] He was interested in knowing what the minimal level of identity difference between groups was required for people to discriminate based on group identity. In other words, he wanted to know how little difference between groups was required before inter-group behaviors were activated.

In one experiment, subjects were asked to estimate the number of dots on a screen and, subsequently, regardless of their actual estimations, some participants were given the group label as 'overestimators' of the dots and others were given the group label as 'underestimators' of the dots. Again, these were random labels providing very minimal

58. Henri Tajfel, "Experiments in Intergroup Discrimination," *Scientific American* 223, no. 5 (1970): 96–103; see, also, Klein, *Why We're Polarized*, 49–55; see Mason, *Uncivil Agreement*, 10–12. See, also, Henri Tajfel, et al., "Social Categorization and Intergroup Behaviour," *European Journal of Social Psychology* 1, no. 2 (1971): 149–178.

group identity, as the actual number of dots named by the subject did not factor into deciding group membership.

In another experiment, subjects were asked to state their preference for certain paintings, though the two artists of the various paintings were not revealed. Therefore, participants did not know which artist they were affirming. They were then given a group identity based on one of two artists' names, regardless of their actual painting preferences. Again, the two groups were randomly created with a minimal, make-believe identity marker.

In both experiments, after being placed in their random and generally meaningless groups, participants were asked to make decisions about distributing sums of fake money to members of their own group or members of the out-group. Their own personal self-interest for gaining money was not in play, as they were only deciding amounts of money that would be given to other people.

What Tajfel found was confounding and defied his own predictions. With just the smallest identity markers possible, which were randomly assigned and quite meaningless, a majority of the subjects chose to give more money to members of their own group and less money to members of the other group. Tajfel also found that when simply asked to give out money without any limits when considering only members of the in-group or only members of the out-group, the in-group, on average, was awarded more. In other words, participants consistently gave the out-group less even if it had no positive benefit for the in-group.

Quite remarkably, in yet another finding, rather than seeking, in all cases, to maximize the money members of their own group would receive, subjects sometimes chose to give their own members less if doing so meant the gap between what the in-group and out-group received was greater. Put another way: participants chose to receive less in order to punish more severely the out-group. According to Tajfel, it was not rewarding the most money to in-group members that was the greatest source of motivation; it was the desire to win, and to punish the out-group in doing so.

At a minimum, these experiments, and many others conducted to test similar group dynamics,[59] show that human beings are wired to view, and respond to, the world in an 'us versus them' mentality.[60] With just minimal group identity markers, people will reward their own group and punish out-group members. People are motivated to have their groups win, even if it means that they themselves will not necessarily gain a reward in doing so, albeit witnessing the out-group lose.

Politics as Us Versus Them

Tajfel's experiments provide a lens to view the political-cultural groups to which people belong today in the United States. If minimal, randomly assigned identity markers influence people to behave in an 'us versus them' mentality, whereby people reward in-group members and punish out-group members, such as was demonstrated in Tajfel's experiments, it is easy to see how these inter-group tendencies can be triggered, and amplified, when the identity markers constituting a group are extremely important to the members. As was previously explored, for many people, nearly all their most important and intimately held identity markers are sorted into, and align with, their political identities. These are not randomly assigned, minimally

---

59. See Klein, *Why We're Polarized*, 55.
60. See Mason's conclusion in *Uncivil Agreement*, 10–12.

important aspects of their life, as was the case with Tajfel's experiments. These identity markers are the very ways that people make meaning of their world, understand their purpose in life, and do so in the context of navigating various forms of fragility. The mega-groups which form around, and support, these markers are extremely important.

From these observations, and based on many of the factors discussed thus far in this book, those who study the challenge of polarization suggest that a helpful analogue for understanding American political polarization is by viewing the two parties (mega-groups) as two 'teams' or 'tribes' competing against each other, holding, in some cases, extremely negative feelings toward the other tribe or team, having very little in common, and competing in ways that reflect a zero-sum game. There exists an 'us versus them' competition taking place where winner takes all, and where the common good is rarely considered. The desire for members, which is more important than anything else, is that the in-group wins, the out-group loses and, if possible, that the out-group is 'punished' in the process.

Miller and Johnston Conover, in the study referred to above, note this observation. They conclude that today "the behavior of partisans resembles that of sports team members acting to preserve the status of their teams rather than thoughtful citizens participating in the political process for the broader good."[61] And just how high are the stakes? In other words, how profoundly do people perceive the threat of the opposing political team? Miller and Johnston Conover continue: "Democrats and Republicans with strong identities perceive the opposing party as rivals who are fundamentally immoral and cannot be trusted;

61. Miller and Conover, "Red and Blue," 225.

likewise, they are enraged at each other for 'destroying American democracy.'"[62]

This latter statement, indicating how intensely negative feelings are felt, invites a deeper look into the reality of 'negative polarization.'

Negative Polarization

Over the last few decades, the rise of negative polarization has occurred in the United States. David French provides a definition of this reality that both enlightens and devastates. He remarks:

> In plain English [the existence of negative polarization] means that a person belongs to their political party not so much because they like their own party but because they hate and fear the other side. Republicans don't embrace Republican policies so much as they despise Democrats and Democratic policies. Democrats don't embrace Democratic policies as much as they vote to defend themselves from Republicans. At this point, huge majorities actively dislike their political opponents and significant minorities see them as possessing subhuman characteristics.[63]

Negative polarization is Tajfel's findings amplified, and manifested, in two sorted, homogenous political-cultural groups, that have little contact and even less in common, and that feel threatened by each other or, worse, hate each other: they desire to see the other 'team' lose, and not just

---

62. Miller and Conover, "Red and Blue," 235.
63. French, *Divided We Fall*, 2.

because they like their own team, but because they hate, fear, do not understand, and despise the other team.[64]

Examples abound depicting the rising hatred of, and animosity directed toward, opposing mega-groups. I do not want to dwell on these behaviors, as doing so may distract from the overall argument of this book, perhaps by triggering the very feelings to which I have been alluding. However, a few examples suffice to depict the issue, and others can be found within Yale professor Amy Chua's well-documented book, *Political Tribes*.

For instance, commenting on the mega-group occupying the heartland of America that most-often votes Republican and is more likely to be populated by Christians, a Silicon Valley executive—i.e., a member of the so-called progressive mega-group—remarked that she and other people 'like her' did not want to live in middle America because: "'[N]o educated person wants to live in a shithole with stupid people" who are "violent, racist, and/or misogynistic..."'[65]

Comments spoken in the other direction are just as vitriolic. Expressing an overall disdain for 'liberal elites,' one conservative political commentator stated: "'Liberals hate America, they hate 'flag-wavers,' they hate abortion opponents, they hate all religious groups except Islam (post 9/11). Even Islamic terrorists don't hate America likes [sic] liberals do.'"[66] From this perspective, out-group members are so despicable that terrorists supersede them in moral authority.

---

64. For a reflection on the animosity felt regarding political opponents, see Rob Vischer, "Our Deepening Polarization," *Mirror of Justice*, October 3, 2021, https://mirrorofjustice.blogs.com/mirrorofjustice/2021/10/our-deepening-polarization.html.

65. This quote is taken from Chua, *Political Tribes*, 163.

66. See Chua, *Political Tribes*, 163.

The rise of negative feelings toward one's rival political party is more than anecdotal and is well-documented in statistical data.[67] For instance, in 1960, 5 percent of Republicans in a survey indicated that they would be upset if their children married a Democrat. That number, in 2008, rose to 27 percent, and in 2010 was 49 percent. For Democrats who would be upset if their child married a Republican the percentages were 4 in 1960, 20 in 2008, and 33 in 2010.

Lilliana Mason documents other evidence of political anger toward an out-group political party.[68] In studying data related to feelings partisans held toward an out-group presidential candidate, she notes that anger toward the out-group candidate has fluctuated based on election cycles but has generally increased over the last few decades. Beginning when the data was made available in 1980, 40 percent of politically aligned voters felt anger toward the out-group presidential candidate. In 2012, the number was 60 percent.

A Pew Research poll documents a similar rise in negative attitudes. For example, in 2016, 61 percent of Democrats held 'unfavorable' views of Republicans and 69 percent of Republicans held 'unfavorable' views of Democrats. Those numbers, in 2019, jumped to 79 percent and 83 percent, respectively. Commenting on these and other trends of rising unfavorability, the article states: "Three years ago, Pew Research Center found that the 2016 presidential campaign was 'unfolding against a backdrop of intense partisan division and animosity.' Today, the level of division and animosity – including negative sentiments among

---

67. See Klein, *Why We're Polarized*, 75–76.
68. Mason, *Uncivil Agreement*, 78–101.

partisans toward the members of the opposing party – has only deepened."[69]

Intensifying Negativity

The final section of this chapter connects to the final section of the previous chapter. Just as it was argued that there are incentives for certain actors in American culture to pursue actions that bring about homogeneity across various cultural spheres that are representative of sorted demographic groups, so there are incentives for certain actors to stoke feelings of rage within members of one mega-group toward those of another group, or to depict out-group members in a negative way. Referring to the working metaphor of this chapter, as the warming of oceans seems to increase the size and strength of some hurricanes, thereby increasing the destruction caused by the hurricane's interaction with most everything, so do certain groups stoking rage, resentment, and negativity within already triggered polarized groups fuel the strength and intensity of negative interactions between groups.

Political parties, for instance, benefit by stoking feelings of rage and resentment among their voters. As was mentioned above, those people most likely to work on behalf of a political party, or those most likely to cast a vote for a party's candidate, are the people who feel the greatest sense of anger toward, fear of, or hatred for, the opposing party.[70] It is tempting, therefore, for politicians

---

69. See Pew Research Center, "Partisan Antipathy: More Intense, More Personal," *Pew Research Center*, October 10, 2019, https://www.pewresearch.org/politics/2019/10/10/partisan-antipathy-more-intense-more-personal/.
70. See Miller and Conover, "Red and Blue."

to stoke these feelings for their own benefit, i.e., to get voters fired-up and ready to work on behalf of the politician by casting the opponent in an increasingly negative light. Klein is clear on this point:

> Politicians, of course, are not equally responsive to all their constituents. They are most concerned about the most enraged: the people who will vote for them, volunteer for them, donate to them. And the way to make more of that kind of voter isn't just to focus on how great you are. It's to focus on how bad the other side is. Nothing brings a group together like a common enemy. Remove the fury and fear of a real opponent, and watch enthusiasm drain from your supporters.[71]

For all intents and purposes, rage motivates, and politicians have an incentive to stimulate those feelings by making the opposing party look worse.

Social media and other traditional media outlets benefit from allowing rage and negativity to fester on their platforms as well.[72] As was referred to in chapter one, the algorithms that direct platforms, such as those used by Facebook, 'reward' posts that attract the most attention, such as 'likes,' comments, or 'shares.' The posts which garner much attention are often negative commentary on political realities, particularly aimed at undermining opposing parties or mega-groups. The more traffic directed toward, and the amount of time spent on, a particular post or story, the more advertising revenue for the social media platform increases. Studying this issue, a Brookings' report indicated: "Facebook is fully aware of

---

71. Klein, Why We're Polarized, 63.
72. See Barrett, "How Tech Platforms." See, also, Lanier, Ten Arguments, 42–56.

how its automated systems [algorithms] promote divisiveness. The company does extensive internal research on the polarization problem and periodically adjusts its algorithms to reduce the flow of content likely to stoke political extremism and hatred. But typically, it dials down the level of incendiary content for only limited periods of time."[73] Rage and negativity are lucrative, and people seek to benefit from them. Meanwhile, the destruction caused by intensifying polarized hurricanes worsens.

What is more, it seems that all people benefit, in some way, from experiencing negativity. For example, research has shown that parts of the brain associated with 'reward centers' tend to be activated when in-group members see out-group members struggle or suffer. Stated differently, when viewing stories, articles, or images that show out-group members struggling or suffering, there is a switch turned on in the brain indicating that people are experiencing pleasure. Commenting on this reality, Amy Chua states that "it seems that schadenfreude has a neurological basis."[74] Ever wonder why it is so addicting to watch biased network news, or watch endless negative videos on YouTube? It turns out that viewing negative depictions of one's opponents can feel good, thereby providing a benefit or incentive for people to view them.

Conclusion

The cultural situation brought about by polarization is bleak. The central metaphor I utilized to highlight this reality was chosen intentionally: hurricanes are beneficial

---

73. See Barrett, "How Tech Platforms."
74. Chua, Political Tribes, 41. Chua is referencing the research of Mina Cikara.

for few, especially when they collide. And polarized hurricanes in the United States are growing, affecting nearly every aspect of people's lives, sucking them into the vortex of negativity, and increasing people's feelings of fragility. In the next chapter, I am going to explore some of the potential problems these hurricanes cause for a particular demographic in the United States: Christians.

Chapter Three

The Church and Polarization

"This is not who I am."

Walmart can be a wild place to shop in normal times. During a hurricane, it's pandemonium.

Days before Hurricane Florence reached the shores of North Carolina, I began preparing for the onslaught. After prematurely ending a spiritual retreat on the Carolina coast, I heeded the advice of locals and set out to buy provisions. Rural America does not offer too many options, so I resigned myself to enter the Walmart extravaganza.

Folks were in panic mode. I had never seen anything like it before. It was Black Friday in September.

People were sprinting—not jogging—sprinting through the store. The young were elbowing the old; the old were chastising the young. One woman was nearly knocked to the floor.

Voices boomed through the air: "Did you find bread?" "There's no milk left!" "Grab that last jug of water!" "Johnny, where'd you go?" "Get over here right now or I'm gonna give you something to cry about!" (Thankfully, she wasn't talking to me!)

Case upon case of water was piled on shopping carts whose wheels were ready to break. Toilet paper was nowhere to be found. Shelves were empty...and I mean empty. People held baskets, pushed carts, and carried food all in one frantic motion.

Standing around and observing the crowds, my adrenaline spiked. Primal survival switches turned on. "Am I going to have enough food? What about water?" I glanced left and right as my heart pounded. Thoughtlessly, I threw what items remained into my cart.

Walking near a woman short in stature, I noticed she could not reach a can of tomatoes on the top shelf. Her gaze caught my eye, imploring my help. I walked on by. It was not my most virtuous moment.

Halfway through 'shopping' I stopped, took a deep breath, and said to myself: "What in the world is going on? What am I doing? This is not who I am."

Indeed, I suspect that for most people running around the store that day, it was not who they were, either. Something about the impending hurricane, the contagious effects of group emotions, and the primal urge for survival had taken ahold of us all. We had become something we were not, and could do little about it.

In many ways, the hurricanes of polarized groups function similarly in American society. The logic of polarization subsumes, forms, and influences us in ways that are nearly unavoidable. I am not saying we lose our freedom to choose otherwise, or that we can do nothing about it. But we often get sucked up into the storm, and are twisted and whirled until we resemble yet another member of a polarized group. Before we know it, we are sharing negative posts on Facebook; hating a particular Church official; critiquing an article from 'that' news outlet before reading it; yelling at the television because they are showing 'that' politician; or peeling out of our driveway in triggered anger because of our neighbor's political yard signs. In no time, polarization shifts from something 'out there' to something working in each of us, as we ourselves are enveloped by the storm.

In this chapter, I am going to look specifically at the Christian demographic of the United States, to investigate how Christians are possibly being subsumed into the hurricanes of polarization. I will attempt to juxtapose ways that the Church has, in the past, lived according to her nature in admirable ways—especially in her saints—with how certain tendencies within polarized culture today can impede Christians from living the demands of the gospel. To ease the reception of this sensitive topic, I will, along the way, provide a kind of 'examination of conscience,' inviting us all, as we are willing, to think about our own lives in light of social and ecclesial polarization, looking first to the 'plank' in our own eye, and only then to the 'slivers' in the eyes of those around us. In so doing, perhaps we, in the Church, can avoid the perpetuation of the logic of polarization, and watch as the hurricanes slowly dissipate, and, hopefully, disappear.

The Church as One, Holy, Catholic, and Apostolic

No age of the Church has been without tension, turmoil, or divisiveness. The fourth century, for example, was a period not unlike our own. There was political upheaval, as the Roman Empire teetered on collapse; struggle for authority and power, as the curtain of Constantine's reign was being lifted; and ecclesial divisiveness—and, yes, polarization—surrounding some of the most fundamental Christian beliefs.[1]

In the height of the tension of the fourth century, the Church, by way of Emperor Theodosius I (347–395), convened a council. Gathered in Constantinople, the fathers of the council, in a creedal statement that built on the Council of Nicaea held just decades earlier, affirmed and proclaimed the Church as one, holy, catholic, and apostolic. From that day, to our own time, professing belief in these marks of the Church reminds Christians that they (the marks) will always exist in the Church, and, because of the Church's divine constitution, they cannot be lost.[2]

Even as these marks remain in the Church, however, the extent to which they are lived, or cultivated, by each Christian varies. The call, therefore, to Christians in every age—which is a missionary mandate—is to proclaim these words, "I believe in one, holy, catholic and apostolic Church," while seeking to manifest what is contained within them more fully—that is, to live them more deeply—through their words and actions. The invitation for all Christians is to cooperate with Jesus' grace in order to make the Church and the world more unified (one), more charitable (holy), more inter-connected within the economy of salvation (catholic), and more deeply rooted in the tradition of the gospel under the leadership of the Church (apostolic).[3]

These four marks will be used as a guide to the following analysis of the contemporary Church in the United

---

1. On this point, see John Vidmar, OP, *The Catholic Church Through the Ages* (New York: Paulist Press, 2005), 55–59.
2. I am indebted to the ecclesiology of Benoît-Dominique de la Soujeole, OP. See *Introduction to the Mystery of the Church*, trans. Michael J. Miller (Washington, DC: The Catholic University of America Press, 2014).
3. See Soujeole, *Introduction to the Mystery*, 515–620.

States and her relationship with (or within) the culture of polarization.

Unity within the Church

The Witness of St. Paul

Pursuing and maintaining unity within the Church has been of utmost importance since the beginning of Christianity. St. Paul (5–65) provides considerable data in this regard. As he was traveling around the ancient world, seeking to establish Christian communities, Paul would relentlessly have to remind the followers of Christ to remain united.

Take the Galatian community, for instance. Ethnicity, gender, and status, among other things, were threatening unity. It is understandable that common human differences such as these would cause some level of division between members of any community. For Paul, however, and for the people of his communities, this was unacceptable. Christians were called to be different. And the unity brought about by life in Christ was to be maintained regardless of the differences or distinctions between individuals. Paul was clear on this point: "There is neither Jew nor Greek, there is neither slave nor free person, there is not male and female; for you are all one in Christ Jesus" (Gal. 3:28).

Paul's theology of ecclesial unity was rooted in his understanding of baptism. According to him, baptism produced a bond between Christians more foundational than any other existing bond. And membership in the Church, which baptism secures, is the identity that should matter most to Christians—it is more important than race, ethnicity, country, or status. Written in the theological tradition of Paul, the letter to the Ephesians confirms this point:

"[Strive] to preserve the unity of the spirit through the bond of peace: one body and one Spirit, as you were also called to the one hope of your call; one Lord, one faith, one baptism; one God and Father of all, who is over all and through all and in all" (Eph. 4:3-6).

In responding to a whole range of issues that were causing divisions in his nascent communities, from liturgical abuses (cf. 1 Cor. 11), to rival voices challenging Paul's own leadership and message (cf. 1 Cor. 1:10-11), or the misunderstanding of spiritual gifts (cf. 1 Cor. 12), the Church's first great missioner was consistent in his message of unity: "I urge you, brothers, in the name of our Lord Jesus Christ, that all of you agree in what you say, and that there be no divisions among you, but that you be united in the same mind and in the same purpose" (1 Cor. 1:10).

A Struggle for Unity in the Church

Given the importance of unity between Christians, that is, the call Christians have received to deepen unity within the Church, the culture of polarization in the United States, which tends toward the formation of mega-group hurricanes that can intensely interact with each other in negative, divisive ways, presents particular problems for American Christians. Polarized hurricanes, if they fester, form, and interact with each other *within the Church*, can undermine the unity that Jesus desires for his followers. Indeed, looking specifically at the Catholic demographic in the US, it appears that hurricanes have formed right in the heart of the Church.[4]

---

4. I am addressing the Catholic Church in this section, as statistics indicate there exists two quite distinct groups of Christians forming within the Catholic Church, based on political preferences. This is

According to a Pew Research report, Catholics in the United States are equally represented in the Republican and Democratic parties, 48 percent, and 47 percent, respectively. There is also racial sorting within these swirling hurricanes, reflecting the demographics explored in chapter one. Most white Catholics identify as Republican (57 percent) while most Hispanic and Black Catholics identify as Democrat (68 percent and 85 percent, respectively).[5] Similar racial sorting within the Church exists for support of presidential candidates. Moreover, support for some policy issues indicates the formation of polarized groups within the Church. Concerning immigration policy, for instance, the numbers are telling: a 2020 poll indicated 81 percent of Catholic Republicans favored expanding the wall at the southern border, while 91 percent of Catholic Democrats opposed it.[6]

It is important to pause to consider a few observations regarding the statistics just presented. To begin, it is possible to have differing political affinities within the Church, and the formation of sorted groups around these affinities, while maintaining unity between Christians.

---

not to deny that other Christian denominations have similar challenges related to polarization. I will, for example, investigate evangelicals more in-depth below. On divisions within the evangelical world, see David Brooks, "The Dissenters Trying to Save Evangelicalism From Itself," *The New York Times*, February 4, 2022, https://www.nytimes.com/2022/02/04/opinion/evangelicalism-division-renewal.html. For another voice concerned with the way politics is affecting evangelical faith, see Stanley, *Not in It to Win It*.

5. Besheer Mohamed, et al., "Religion and Politics," *Pew Research Center*, February 16, 2021, https://www.pewforum.org/2021/02/16/religion-and-politics/. Gregory A. Smith, "Facts about Catholics and Politics in the U.S.," *Pew Research Center*, September 15, 2020, https://www.pewresearch.org/fact-tank/2020/09/15/8-facts-about-catholics-and-politics-in-the-u-s/.

6. Smith, "Facts about Catholics."

Further research, especially qualitative sociological research, is required to understand the level to which sorted groups in the Church are interacting in divisive ways that threaten unity.[7]

Anecdotally, however, by way of stories shared from local parishes and churches, especially from ministers and priests of those communities, it does seem that bonds of unity are being threatened within the Church.[8] Many ministers I talk to speak in exasperation, particularly during election cycles, of how challenging it is to lead polarized communities. They find it difficult to preach without being accused, one way or the other, of supporting a particular political party. Others speak of whole groups of parishioners leaving their parish *en mass* after a falling out with another group. Polarization can be seen, as well, when Catholic media outlets report quite different interpretations of the events concerning various ecclesial leaders.[9] And, based on the research presented in

---

7. On this point, see Mary Ellen Konieczny, et al., ed., *Polarization in the US Catholic Church: Naming the Wounds, Beginning to Heal* (Collegeville: Liturgical Press, 2016).

8. On this point, see Michael J. O'Loughlin, "Catholic Leaders Confront Polarization but Skirt Polarizing Issues at Georgetown Forum," *American Magazine*, June 8, 2018, https://www.americamagazine. org/faith/2018/06/08/catholic-leaders-confront-polarization-skirt-polarizing-issues-georgetown-forum.

9. See this source for more on this topic: The Pillar, "The Pillar Podcast Ep. 36: The Pope and the Platypus," *The Pillar Podcast*, September 17, 2021, https://www.pillarcatholic.com/p/the-pillar-podcast-ep-36-the-pope?utm_source=url. See, also, Robert David Sullivan, "The Most-Viewed Stories of 2021: The Latin Mass, Pope Francis vs. EWTN and Covid-19 (again)," *America Magazine*, December 29, 2021, https://www.americamagazine.org/politics-society/2021/12/29/pope-francis-latin-mass-ewtn-242108. Other stories that have brought about wildly different coverage have been the various Catholic Synods, especially the Synod of Bishops for Pan-Amazon Region. One can do a simple search in *First Things* or *America Magazine* and find quite different coverage.

chapters one and two regarding the nature of in-group and out-group rivalry, and the way in which political identities have become mega-identities, wherein political culture affects most aspects of people's life, it is safe to assume that polarized hurricanes are intensifying within the Church. The Catholic Church appears well situated to be a microcosm of the macro-political scene in the United States.[10]

The extent to which Christians can maintain unity with these differences, that is, with the existence of polarized groups within the Church, harkens back to Paul's invitation to unity for the early Christian communities. One can be, for instance, a fully believing and practicing Catholic and support a Democratic candidate while still appreciating, listening to, and loving a member of the Republican Party who is also Catholic, and vice versa. Negative and vitriolic political culture does not have to determine relationships between Christians. Catholic Democrats and Catholic Republicans can worship together and work toward fulfilling God's will together. They can recognize their mutual baptismal bonds, and subordinate other personal identities (especially their political identity) to their Christian identity.

Another observation is that there may be certain issues that Catholics or other Christians *will want to* be polarized around, even within the Church.[11] For example,

---

10. See Matt Malone, S.J., "Who is the Cause of Society's Polarization? All of Us." *American Magazine*, April 20, 2018, https://www.america-magazine.org/politics-society/2018/04/20/who-cause-societys-polarization-all-us.

11. Klein argues that, in regards to certain values or policy issues, people of good will should polarize around issues related to justice, particularly if there are groups pushing ideas that promote injustice. See *Why We're Polarized*, 249–251. Of course, the nuances of what constitutes justice become important.

if there is a hypothetical sect within the Christian Church that holds that Canadians should be jailed and tortured in American facilities, that the United States should invade and appropriate Canada, and that the US military should kill any Canadians who oppose this effort, Christians should rightly join together in ways that counter this movement. Christians, it seems, should be polarized (sorted, thinking similarly, and energized) around a group that opposes this obviously (I hope) immoral geopolitical stance.

There are likely certain policy positions—often, though not exclusively, those policies related to 'life issues' and to the preservation of human dignity—that Christians today feel rightly justified in supporting, even if doing so increases a certain kind of polarization (again, my purpose here is not to debate particular policy issues). If the choice to polarize around a particular issue is discerned, Christians need to consider how they engage those Christians with different perspectives, while seeking to maintain the love and unity essential to Christianity.[12] Furthermore, Christians, in a situation where they choose to unite around a particular pole of an issue for the sake of justice, will need to seek to be formed by the entirety of the Church's social tradition, and not just the elements of the tradition that harmonize with their political party (more on this below).[13] In other words, one's passion for,

---

12. See Sara Stewart Holland and Beth Silvers, *I Think You're Wrong (But I'm Listening): A Guide to Grace-Filled Political Conversations* (Nashville: Nelson Books, 2019). For two articles that address engaging the other 'side' on 'life issues,' see R.J. Snell, "Three Tasks After Roe," *Public Discourse: The Journal of the Witherspoon Institute*, May 27, 2022, https://www.thepublicdiscourse.com/featured/three-tasks-after-roe/. See, also, Julia D. Hejduk, "Seeing Beyond Roe," *Public Discourse: The Journal of the Witherspoon Institute*, October 29, 2020, https://www.thepublicdiscourse.com/2020/10/72325/.

13. On this point, see Erin Stoyell-Mulholland, "Polarization and Abor-

and commitment to, a particular policy issue—no matter how important the issue is—should not impede one from embracing, and seeking to live, the entirety of the Church's social teaching. Neither should they (one's passion and commitment) create irreconcilable enemies between members of the Body of Christ.

What is germane to this examination regarding unity is whether, and to what extent, one's behavior either deepens unity between Christians or threatens division. Some of the following questions may be helpful to consider.

When I cast a vote for a political candidate, do I consider the importance of my unity with Christians who perhaps cast a different vote? When I am about to share a political post on social media, am I haunted by the overwhelming evidence in the Christian tradition that calls me to be a person who promotes unity within the Body of Christ?

Do I regulate the amount of time I spend watching media outlets whose business model rests on creating division and intensifying animosity? Do I spend time praying over Paul's endless exhortations for unity?

Do I recognize that my Christian identity, flowing from my baptism, is more important than any other aspect of my identity—that neither family, race, nation, political persuasion, geography, or personal theological or liturgical preferences—are more important than this fundamental identity?

If I am a Christian leader, a minister, pastor or priest, do I, like Paul, humble myself and deny my own desire for popularity, fame, gratification, or employment, and strive to maintain unity in all my actions and words, despite my own political views or personality traits?

tion: Living Out Our Pro-Life Beliefs," in *Polarization in the US Catholic Church*, 119–129.

94

These questions are vital for considering unity *within* the Church. Also important to the Church is unity with the world. This is the subject of the following section.

Unity with the World

The Witness of St. Francis

To profess that the Church is one also implies that part of the mission of the Church is to promote unity among all people, including unity with non-Christians.[14] Many figures in the Christian tradition are astounding witnesses to this task. The well-known thirteenth century saint of Assisi, Francis, a cherished figure in the Catholic, Protestant, and non-Christian world, shines among them.[15]

To understand the remarkable, even countercultural, commitment to unity of *Il Poverello*, as he was nicknamed, it is necessary to transport ourselves to the medieval European world. Only by briefly imagining part of the

14. On this point, see Henri de Lubac, *Catholicism: Christ and the Common Destiny of Man*, trans. Lancelot C. Sheppard and Sister Elizabeth Englund, OCD (San Francisco: Ignatius, 1988).
15. On Saint Francis, see Robert Barron, *The Pivotal Players: 12 Heroes Who Shaped the Church and Changed the World* (Park Ridge: Word on Fire, 2020), 43–59. See, also, G.K. Chesterton, *St. Francis of Assisi* (London: Hodder and Soughton LTD, n.d.). Accessed online through The Project Gutenberg at https://www.gutenberg.org/files/63084/63084-h/63084-h.htm. I admit that one of the weaknesses of this chapter is that I do not provide more examples of Protestant saintly witnesses. My hope in choosing St. Paul and St. Francis, however, is that Protestants do feel some connection to them. What is more, I will be covering the life of Dietrich Bonhoeffer below, and, moreover, I utilize the writings of other Protestant figures throughout this text. These figures have written splendidly on issues related to polarization. I thank my Protestant brothers and sisters for their understanding, and I hope that my central focus on Jesus Christ provides ample content for consideration.

world of St. Francis can his radical commitment to unity be fully appreciated.

During the medieval period in Europe, the fortress, with its impregnable bastions, captured people's imaginations.[16] Royalty, aristocracy, courtiers, clergy, and other people of importance sought to build for themselves various types of fortresses for protection—castles, monasteries, and towns—surrounded by diverse sorts of bastions, often including towers and turrets. Along with these more influential people of status, many others sought to live within, and to expand, fortresses to enjoy the relative safety of the stone or wood that kept out anything unwanted. If one did not have the luxury to be within the bastions, there was increased danger from isolation, the possibility of being exposed to enemies, and a greater likelihood of death.

In the medieval mind, the idea of the fortress with bastions was applied to geography, as well. Centuries of barbarian invasions required Europeans to think of their land as one grand fortress. Within this mindset, it was imagined that, in order to protect those within a geographic area, it was necessary to defend the 'geographic fortress,' defeat and push back enemies from a region, and extend and strengthen the bastions to include more land within an area. This expansionist vision of the fortress could even be called a kind of 'geopolitical' stance maintained by leaders. The subsequent rise of Islam, and the nearly ever-present battles and crusades that Christians engaged in with Muslims, only solidified this vision.[17]

---

16. See Hans Urs von Balthasar, *Razing the Bastions: On the Church in this Age*, trans. Brian McNeil (San Francisco: Ignatius Press, 1993). See, also, J.B. Bury, *The Cambridge Medieval History* (New York: Macmillan, 1936).

17. For some helpful resources, see Jonathan Riley-Smith, *The Crusades, Christianity, and Islam* (New York: Columbia University Press, 2011);

And then came St. Francis.

The gentle man from Assisi was no stranger to military endeavors. Neither was he naïve concerning the violence that existed from the clash between Christians and Muslims. He knew what was at stake in these conflicts. The world, as it was known to Europeans of his time, was at war. People were dying. Values and beliefs were threatened. Everything hung in the balance.

It was his courage and creativity, however, in the face of turbulence, which made him an exemplary witness to the Church's pursuit of unity with the non-Christian world. When most people thought creating and fortifying bastions were the only way to secure the Church's future and respond to the outsider, Francis creatively decided to step over those bastions, walk into the threat, and engage the so-called enemy in conversation.

As the story goes, Francis journeyed to the Christian-Muslim fighting lines at Damietta in the Nile Delta. After spending time with the Christian forces, he approached the geographical bastions—the battle lines. He walked toward the Muslim forces, was captured, and was brought before the Sultan. Engaging the Sultan, Francis spoke of his faith, was willing to demonstrate what he believed to be true, invited the Sultan to consider Jesus, listened, and, ultimately (to the shock of many, including Francis), was released.

It is difficult to know exactly what followed from the exchange, but tradition holds that a mutual sharing and reception of gifts took place between Francis and the Sultan. Francis, on the one hand, learned much from

---

Benjamin Z. Kedar, *Crusade and Mission: European Approaches toward the Muslims* (Princeton: Princeton University Press, 1984); and Thomas F. Madden, "Inventing the Crusades," *First Things* 194 (2009): 41–44.

the Sultan and appreciated the wisdom offered to him.[18] The Sultan, on the other hand, was quite impressed with Francis. Some writers suggest that, were it not for his commitment to his own family and people, the Sultan would have accepted faith in Jesus Christ.[19]

Even without knowing all the details, the exchange between the two is hailed today as a precursor to the way in which the Church can engage the non-Christian world in ways that are "honest, clear, nonviolent, and mutually respectful."[20] When most of the Christian world thought the only way forward when engaging Islam and other perceived threats was creating geographical bastions, fortifying the fortress, and defeating the other in conflict, Francis proposed and exemplified crossing over, engaging in conversation, and risking one's life in doing so, in order to bring faith to, and unity in, the world.

A Struggle for Unity with the World

There are a number of similarities that can be drawn between the polarized situation of America and the conflicted period encountered by Francis in the thirteenth century. The geographic, cultural, and identity-based sorting of the United States are creating metaphorical bastions between polarized groups—one predominantly Christian, the other not. People living in different areas of the United States, belonging to different races, and maintaining quite

---

18. On this point, see Paul Moses, *The Saint and the Sultan: The Crusades, Islam, and Francis of Assisi's Mission of Peace* (New York: Doubleday Religion, 2009).

19. Barron, *The Pivotal Players*, 55–56. See, also, Chesterton, *St. Francis*, 147–149.

20. See Barron, *The Pivotal Players*, 56. See, also, Chesterton, *St. Francis*, 141–143.

different metaphysical views of the world, are rarely coming in contact or interacting. Like Francis' time, where there was not an overabundance of engagement between Muslims and Christians except for purposes of conflict, today, there is little engagement between polarized groups unless of the negative kind. And, as will be explored more thoroughly in the next chapter, in ways that reflect the mindset of Francis' time, the dominant metaphor utilized to inform engagement between polarized groups in the present moment, especially by many Christians, is that of war—a 'culture war.'[21]

For Christians, who are called to deepen unity between all people, the existence of permanent, impregnable bastions—whether of the military, ideological, or geographical type—between them and any demographic group, presents problems. This is not to say that borders are unimportant, or that there will not be understandable, and sometimes quite irreconcilable, differences between Christians and non-Christians. But Christians cannot be satisfied being separated by bastions with the out-group world if that separation hinders their missionary movement. Jesus directs his followers to go to 'the nations,' engaging with people from all backgrounds, creeds, races, or politics, bringing the gifts of the Church to others who have never encountered them (Mt. 28: 16-20), and loving 'the other' even to the point of giving up one's life (Jn. 15:13).

Considering the various Christian denominations in the United States, the potential for creating bastions seems to be the most acute for evangelicals.[22]

---

21. See, for instance, Andrew Hartman, A War for the Soul of America: A History of the Culture Wars, 2nd ed. (Chicago: University of Chicago Press, 2019).

22. For more on evangelicals, see the site: https://www.nae.org/what-is-an-evangelical/. I am not an evangelical, but am friends, and

Evangelicals appear to be forming a generally homogenous group (though with some diversity) around one specific political party—the Republican Party—with the potential for either conflict, or disengagement, with outgroup members who share little in common with them.[23] This challenge was particularly revealed in the 2016 Presidential election when, for instance, a staggering 77 percent of white evangelicals voted for Trump, while only 16 percent voted for Clinton.[24] Proportional support for Trump *grew* in 2020 among white evangelicals, in which 84 percent voted for Trump while only 15 percent voted for Biden.[25] Solidifying this political-religious mega-group is a lack of racial and geographic diversity, with 76 percent of self-identifying evangelicals being white, a low percent-

have collaborated in ministry, with many evangelicals. I write these words with the utmost sincerity and respect. Russell Moore discusses some of the following thoughts on *The Ezra Klein Show*. See *The Ezra Klein Show*, "Why the Evangelical Movement Is in 'Disarray' After Dobbs," *The Ezra Klein Show*, August 23, 2022, https://www.nytimes.com/2022/08/23/opinion/ezra-klein-podcast-russell-moore.html.

23. For evangelical voices who share some of the following concerns, and are seeking to understand the present state of evangelicalism, see Jesse Covington, et al., "Hopeful Realism: Renewing Evangelical Political Morality," *Public Discourse: The Journal of the Witherspoon Institute*, July 21, 2022, https://www.thepublicdiscourse.com/2022/07/83450/. See, also, Jordan J. Ballor, et al., "Three Responses to 'Hopeful Realism,'" *Public Discourse: The Journal of the Witherspoon Institute*, July 24, 2022, https://www.thepublicdiscourse.com/2022/07/83584/.

24. Jessica Martínez and Gregory A. Smith, "How the Faithful Voted: A Preliminary 2016 Analysis," *Pew Research Center*, November 9, 2016, https://www.pewresearch.org/fact-tank/2016/11/09/how-the-faithful-voted-a-preliminary-2016-analysis/.

25. Justin Nortey, "Most White Americans Who Regularly Attend Worship Services Voted for Trump in 2020," *Pew Research Center*, August 30, 2021, https://www.pewresearch.org/fact-tank/2021/08/30/most-white-americans-who-regularly-attend-worship-services-voted-for-trump-in-2020/.

age of evangelicals being immigrants (9 percent), and with most white evangelicals concentrated in the south and southeast of the United States—areas with low religious diversity in general, and low 'unaffiliated' religious identity, in particular.[26]

Again, it is important to pause to make a few observations regarding these statistics.

Clearly, the evangelical community attempts to be mission-minded. I have attended the Southern Baptist Convention, for instance, and been inspired by their commitment to church-planting and overseas missions.[27] I have listened in awe to the preaching of Billy Graham (1918–2018), and witnessed the countless hearts he reached for Christ, including those of many people I know personally. I am moved by stories of the various religious awakenings and revivals in the American context motivated by evangelical voices.[28] And I am inspired by evangelical figures who have called for, and promoted, unity.[29] There is no doubt that evangelicals are committed to sharing the gospel, at least in theory, with others who are not like them. Given this 'mission-minded' mentality, therefore, the for-

---

26. PRRI Staff, "The 2020 Census of American Religion," *Public Religion Research Institute*, July 8, 2021, https://www.prri.org/research/2020-census-of-american-religion/. See, also, "Religious Landscape Study: Evangelical Protestants," *Pew Research Center*, https://www.pewforum.org/religious-landscape-study/religious-tradition/evangelical-protestant/.

27. Visit the following site for more information on the convention: https://www.sbc.net.

28. See, for instance, Thomas S. Kidd, *The Great Awakening: The Roots of Evangelical Christianity in Colonial America* (New Haven: Yale University Press, 2007); Sydney Ahlstrom, *A Religious History of the American People* (New Haven: Yale University Press, 1972).

29. For insights into this history, see Douglas A. Foster, et al., ed., *The Encyclopedia of the Stone-Campbell Movement* (Grand Rapids: Eerdmans, 2012).

mation of an evangelical-Republican mega-group does not necessarily imply that evangelicals are not engaging their political out-group. Neither does this imply that engagement with the political or racial other must be necessarily negative and vitriolic.

Nevertheless, the statistical demographic makeup of evangelical Christians, along with their particular geographical distribution in the United States, does suggest that evangelicals will simply not have as much interaction with people of different races, political ideologies, religious beliefs, or cultural interests, unless there is a concerted, ongoing, and intentional effort to do so. Simply living one's life and faith in-place, for evangelicals, will not produce robust engagement with, for instance, non-Christian progressives, self-identifying atheists, or agnostics potentially seeking the divine, because so few live in the areas where evangelicals reside. Even when there is some diversity, particularly racial, within a specific locale that is significantly populated by evangelicals, one of the most segregated times of the week is Sunday morning, when people of color often attend one church, while white evangelicals attend their own.[30] As familiarity with particular demographic groups can enhance one's interaction with the out-group other, there is a substantial risk that evangelicals will struggle to build unity with people with whom they share little in common or have little interaction.[31]

---

30. Cathy Lynn Grossman, "Sunday is Still the Most Segregated Day of the Week," America Magazine, January 16, 2015, https://www.americamagazine.org/content/all-things/sunday-still-most-segregated-day-week.

31. See Anthony J. Gittins, Living Mission Interculturally: Faith, Culture, and the Renewal of Praxis (Collegeville: Liturgical Press, 2015). Furthermore, the research of Tajfel and Chua, as discussed in chapter two, serves as a warning of the power of in-group and out-group tensions and hatred.

Furthermore, given the reality of group dynamics, especially the way in which 'outsiders' begin to be perceived as 'hostile threats,' and given the way in which some conservative-leaning media outlets paint the outsider—particularly the liberal, non-believing, coastal, urbanite—as a threat, there is a risk that this demographic is, or will be, perceived by evangelicals, as the so-called 'enemy.'[32] If this is the mentality shared by even a few, it could be very easy for evangelicals to discern (wrongly) that the only recourse is to create bastions, and to engage the other *as enemy*, in order to protect and secure one's safety, and the safety and Christian identity of one's family.

I know that many goodwilled evangelicals and others share many of the concerns stated above and are working to improve the situation.[33] Moreover, these concerns should not be exclusively for evangelicals: All Christians are called to cultivate unity with the world. As this chapter is to serve as a kind of examination of conscience, the following questions are presented to help facilitate this process.

Do I as a Christian have a deep concern for, and a desire to know and love, out-group members, especially non-Christian agnostics or atheists living in the United States? Does this concern manifest itself in creative methods of crossing over the so-called bastions in order to engage, encounter, dialogue with, and even risk my life for, the out-group other, so that deeper unity might be shared by all?

---

32. Alan Jacobs, *How to Think: A Survival Guide for a World at Odds* (New York: Crown Publishing, 2017), 26–27.

33. See, for instance, the insights from Gary B. Agee, *That We May Be One: Practicing Unity in a Divided Church* (Grand Rapids: Eerdmans, 2022). See, also, Stanley, *Not in It to Win It*. See the various sources noted above, as well.

Has the missionary spirit of the Church waned in recent years? Have I become complacent and comfortable in my sorted, homogeneous group? How am I adapting to the reality that mission is no longer simply something that exists in other countries, but that mission is something that happens in the United States, neighbor to neighbor, or one political mega-group to the other political mega-group?

Do I see the political 'other' as my enemy, and does this view impede me from sharing the love, peace, and unity of Jesus Christ with them?

This last question invites a closer look at what people in the United States find as repugnant in others, and whether Christians are responding in charity to 'repugnance.'

The Church and Holiness

The Witness of St. Damien of Molokai

Living Christian charity is the epitome of holiness. And charity, which is the form of all the virtues, is most especially exemplified in the person who is willing to lay down her life for another (Jn. 15:13). Doing this for a person one already cares for—i.e., sacrificing for, and loving people to the point of giving up one's life for them—is difficult enough. Laying down one's life for someone a person views as repugnant, no matter the cause of the repugnance, is attained by few. And yet, there are glimpses of this kind of selfless charity provided by men and women throughout the 2000-year-old history of Christianity (these virtuous actions are, of course, not limited to Christians).

One man, St. Damien of Molokai (1840–1889), who was given the title 'The Martyr of Charity,' reminds Christians of what it means for the Church to be, and to become, holy— that is, to embrace in love the so-called 'repugnant other,' even if doing so requires one to lay down one's own life.[34] To appreciate the radical witness to charity—and therefore, sanctity—that Jozef De Veuster, as Damien was called at birth, provides for the Church, it is necessary to reflect, as unsatisfying as it may be, on the disease of leprosy.

Leprosy (Hansen's disease) is a horrible disease. Up until the nineteenth and twentieth centuries, little was known about it beyond the symptoms, and no cure existed until the 1940s. Untreated, it causes skin lesions, face, joint, and other bodily deformations, nerve loss and the loss of other sensations, muscle atrophy, eye problems, and painful, disfiguring infections.

The person with leprosy, if the disease is left untreated, can be, in many cases, difficult to gaze upon, because of the horrible effects of the disease. Most people today have an image of the leprous individual as a zombie-like figure, with limbs deformed, fingers missing, wounds foul and festering, and dirty cloths attempting to cover and absorb the pain. For most of history, contraction of this disease meant a life stricken with loss.

Perhaps worse than the physical symptoms of leprosy were the social and religious stigmas that accompanied it because so little was known about the disease and so many feared it. Lepers were outcasts, shunned by society, not even permitted to look upon other human beings, and considered no better or perhaps less than wild animals. What is more, people often viewed leprosy as a kind of punishment for a person's actions, a way in which a vindictive God or power of the universe exacted retribution for a person's or family's iniquities. People did not associate

---

34. May Quinlan, *Damien of Molokai* (London: MacDonald and Evans, 1909); Margaret Bunson and Matthew Bunson, St. *Damien of Molokai: Apostle of the Exiled* (Huntington: Our Sunday Visitor: 2009).

with lepers, not only for fear of the disease, but, also, for fear they would incur similar punishment from God. It was for many of these reasons that the so-called leper colony emerged, a locale where lepers would go to suffer and, ultimately, die, excluded from society.

One such colony existed on the island of Molokai in the present-day state of Hawaii. Out of fear of the disease, and of the desire to protect others from infection, lepers were sent to Molokai, to the colony of Kalawao, beginning in 1866. The living conditions were pitiable—this was no island paradise. The ragged cliffs and vast seas were more like prison walls than Edenic landscapes. The colony was to be provided provisions, including medical care, and it was even understood that it would become self-sufficient, with the people growing their own food. The reality, however, was a dire situation, with food in short supply, deplorable housing, minimal medical care, and nearly nonexistent spiritual sustenance.

It was to these outcasts, these people viewed as repugnant by most of the world, that Pater Damien, inspired by his love of Jesus, would give his life.

Traveling from his home country of Belgium and arriving on the island in 1873, the Apostle to the Exiled would have witnessed a scene few horror movies could capture. One biographer depicts the island's welcome as follows:

> Coming closer to the island we see them [the lepers] in all their horror. They stand out like creatures from some under-world; so brutalised, so hideous, so awful, that they appear to have lost all semblance of human kind. In and out, they creep among the rocks, for some are weak and ill with disease. Others, whose

limbs have dropped off from the rotting joints, crawl along the ground like the brute beasts.[35]

To embrace the situation described above, Damien could only have been motivated by a supernatural charity flowing from his faith. Not only was he willing to love and serve those plagued by this sickness, but he was also willing to risk his own exposure to the disease.

In 1889, nearly 16 years after stepping foot on the island of Molokai, Damien would contract leprosy, and later die with those he came to serve and love.

A Struggle for Holiness in the Church

It might seem that the situation encountered by St. Damien on the island of Molokai is far-removed from the present polarized milieu of the United States. However, every age has social pariahs, outcasts, or people perceived as the 'repugnant other.' Nearly every age, and every group within that age, has a 'them,' the ones to avoid. It seems that today, rather than viewing lepers as those unworthy of social inclusion, the culture of polarization is influencing people, including those in the Church, to see one's political out-group as the 'repugnant cultural other.' No doubt, there are differences between lepers who suffer from a disease they often are not responsible for acquiring, and those who freely choose to espouse political opinions or ideological positions. Nevertheless, Christian discipleship, ideally, requires a response of charity, no matter what one finds repugnant in the other.

In his book *How to Think*, Alan Jacobs investigates the sociological concept of the repugnant cultural other

---

35. Quinlan, *Damien of Molokai*, 80.

(RCO).[36] The RCO is the person an individual loathes, is suspicious of, feels an antagonism toward, and will do virtually anything to avoid. This RCO is the contemporary ideological or political leper. As Jacobs states: "Everyone today seems to have an RCO, and everyone's RCO is on social media somewhere. We may be able to avoid listening to our RCO, but we can't avoid the realization that he or she is out there, shouting from two rooms away." He continues: "This is a profoundly unhealthy situation. It's unhealthy because it prevents us from recognizing others as our neighbors—even when they are quite literally our neighbors."[37]

There are many examples today of the RCO, and each mega-group has their own. Jacobs, for instance, notes that, for liberal academics in particular, and progressives, in general, the RCO is often the fundamentalist or evangelical Christian, frequently residing in rural America.[38] He states that the reverse is also true, wherein the progressive academic at an elite institution is the so-called person of suspicion for the evangelical, as was briefly explored above.[39] Moreover, research suggests (chapter two) that negative feelings of Democrats and Republicans toward the opposite party have increased to quite-unprecedented levels, espe-

---

36. This concept is rooted in the work of Susan Friend Harding. See "Representing Fundamentalism: The Problem of the Repugnant Cultural Other," *Social Research* 58, no. 2 (1991): 373–393. See, also, *The Book of Jerry Falwell: Fundamentalist Language and Politics* (Princeton: Princeton University Press, 2000). See Jacobs, *How to Think*, especially at 26–30.
37. Jacobs, *How to Think*, 27.
38. See Nick Bowlin, "Joke's on Them: How Democrats Gave Up on Rural America," *The Guardian*, February 22, 2022, https://www.theguardian.com/us-news/2022/feb/22/us-politics-rural-america. See, also, Isenberg, *White Trash*.
39. Jacobs, *How to Think*, 26–30.

cially by those actively engaged in politics. These groups see each other as having subhuman characteristics. Many people have likely had the experience of talking to a friend or family member and, after a brief mention of the name of a particular politician or news host, they turn from amiable to irate in nanoseconds. What is more, and perhaps most disturbing, the existence of racial repugnance has a long, dark history in the United States, which continues to show deep in-group and out-group animus.

Within the Catholic world specifically, I have witnessed how the very mention of the name of a particular pope can cause tenured academics to turn red in the face, begin shouting and spouting off every conceivable *ad hominem* they can think of, all in front of a room filled with other professionals. Regarding Catholics in the pews, references to different popes or popular leaders in the Church cause some to glare in hatred, and even to walk out during mass. So-called Catholic Twitter has become a place where revealing one's feelings of repugnance is rarely held back.[40] And evangelicals are trying desperately to deal with similar feelings among their ranks.[41] The RCO is alive and thriving in the polarized situation of the United States.

I would like to pause and highlight the seriousness of this problem. It is not just the fact that having an RCO is contrary to the charity demanded by the gospel; as an ever-present human sin, labeling a group as repugnant has often resulted in genocide.[42] This does not happen in

---

40. The Pillar, "Who is Responsible for These Controversial Twitter Priests?" *The Pillar*, February 1, 2021, https://www.pillarcatholic.com/p/who-is-responsible-for-americas-controversial?utm_source=url.

41. See Brooks, "The Dissenters."

42. See, for instance, Immaculée Ilibagiza, *Left to Tell: Discovering God*

every case, of course. But this tendency is not something that any human beings, especially Christians, should be willing to tolerate. The consequences can be dire. And the scandal of this mentality grows when Christians hold other members of the Body of Christ as repugnant and unworthy of the grace won by Jesus Christ.

Given the urgency of this problem, personal reflection concerning one's own RCO seems necessary.

Do I have a repugnant cultural other? Why has this person or group of people become repugnant to me? Do I find joy when my RCO suffers or is publicly shamed? Have I trolled an RCO online, or 'unfriended' her in a fit of anger? Do I feel the demands of Christian charity to seek God's grace to help me overcome the negative feelings I have regarding this person, even if she seems to be unwilling to dialogue or to consider my position? How might God's healing presence be necessary in my life?

Do I recognize that my own vicious treatment of my RCO participates, however minimally, in the same logic of exclusion and prejudice that has caused millions of genocidal deaths throughout history? Have I familiarized myself with the untold stories of those who have suffered these experiences of exclusion and even murder?

Recognizing that prudence is necessary in applying any demand of the gospel, have I considered how I might approach, or stand in solidarity with, the 'repugnant one,' reflecting the example of St. Damien? Am I willing to learn from the one I despise?

These latter questions invite a further look at the way in which the culture of polarization affects the way people think. It is to this theme that I now turn.

Amidst the Rwandan Holocaust (Carlsbad: Hay House, 2014).

The Church as 'Catholic'

The Witness of St. Thomas Aquinas

To say that Christians are to be 'catholic' and to promote 'catholicity,' means recognizing that the disciples of Jesus are called to remain open to the whole of reality, curiously engaging the world around them. As they engage the world through a 'catholic' approach, they are called to think about, and demonstrate to others, how all that is in creation is situated within the economy of salvation. Said differently, the Church's task, because she is 'catholic,' is to engage with everything—people, ideas, art, culture, and philosophies—to recognize what is true, good, and beautiful within them, and to show how these are related to, and can be amplified by, Christian faith. Rather than closing one's mind, being a Christian can induce a sense of awe that opens a person to the vast mystery of the world.[43]

From the earliest days of Christianity, there have been exemplary figures who have maintained a 'catholic' approach to the world.[44] St. Justin Martyr (100–165), for instance, winnowed non-Christian philosophies to uncover the 'seeds of the word,' i.e., the many truths within philosophical systems that anticipated, and even clarified, aspects of the Christian faith. Other Christians, including those with a specifically missionary vocation, such as Matteo Ricci (1552–1610) of the Society of Jesus, would investigate cultures heretofore novel to Christianity, seeking the wisdom and beauty they contained. Other figures,

---

43. See Robert Barron, "Religion and the Opening Up of the Mind," *Talks at Google*, May 17, 2018, https://www.youtube.com/watch?v=enDhX49F3XI.

44. See Stephan B. Bevans and Roger P. Schroeder, *Constants in Context: A Theology of Mission for Today* (Maryknoll: Orbis Books, 2004).

such as C.S. Lewis (1898–1963), would identify the existential longings, and pressing questions, of a generation,
and respond to them by utilizing the Christian tradition.[45]
Perhaps no figure in the history of Christianity, however,
has exemplified the spirit of 'catholicity' as St. Thomas
Aquinas (1225–1274).[46]

The Angelic Doctor is regarded as one of the most
influential thinkers in the Christian tradition in particular,
and one of the most profound figures of Western culture,
in general. No theologian, save perhaps St. Augustine (354–
430), would leave such an indelible mark on the intellectual
thought of the Church. Libraries are filled with books by,
and about, the 'Ox that Roared.' Regardless of whether a
person considers herself a disciple of Thomas—or even
a Christian, for that matter—for any serious intellectual,
Aquinas' oeuvre is quite nearly unavoidable. Perhaps just
as important as his thought, however, is the model he provides the Church of a 'catholic' approach to the world.

To say that Aquinas had a 'catholic' mind means that
he engaged charitably most all ideas and interlocutors he
encountered, searching for wisdom and knowledge within
them. His was an intensely curious mind, trying to understand all things in light of their relationship to God. When
he encountered a thinker he disagreed with, he treated
them with respect, often bolstering aspects of their arguments while still presenting a different perspective.

Writing on the method in which Thomas approached
the world around him, Robert Barron, a scholar of the
thirteenth-century theologian, states:

---

45. See, for example, C.S. Lewis, *Mere Christianity* (New York: Harper-
One, 2015).
46. See G.K. Chesterton, *St. Thomas Aquinas* (New York: Sheed and
Ward, Inc., 1933).

[Aquinas] beautifully exemplified a truly catholic mind—by which I mean, a mind open to every and any influence, willing to embrace the truth wherever he found it. Thomas was primarily inspired of course by the Bible and the great Christian theological tradition. But he also read and cited with enthusiasm the pagan philosophers Plato, Aristotle, and Cicero; the Jewish rabbi Moses Maimonides; the Muslim scholars Averroes and Avicenna.[47]

Even when his 'catholic' approach to the world threatened his own reputation, Thomas did not cease to discern the existence of wisdom or truth in unlikely places. This was especially the case with his engagement with Aristotle (384–322 BC), who had become a kind of RCO for some in the medieval period. Aquinas disregarded those who held a bias against Aristotle, approached his work in a catholic spirit, and enriched the Church's theological tradition by doing so. In this way, and others, he continues to inspire today.

A Struggle for a 'Catholic' Mind Today

There are many ways in which today's culture of polarization can detract from Christians maintaining a 'catholic' mind. Recalling the research of chapters one and two, the various forms of sorting constitutive of polarization limit people's ability to engage with a diverse set of ideas, philosophies, people, and approaches to life, simply because people from various groups rarely, or sometimes never, interact. It is an exceptional person who intentionally reads a news source they disagree with, or approaches a

---

47. Barron, The Pivotal Players, 77.

group—from another religious background, for example—
with whom they have little in common, in order to engage
in dialogue with, and learn from, them.[48] Opportunities
exist, at least to the extent that the Internet provides many
options, and that Americans are mobile, but people often
become complacent in the comfort of their mega-groups,
or they simply do not think about the need to pursue
other perspectives.

There are also various types of 'cognitive biases' that
are induced, or strengthened, by participation in one's
political-cultural mega-group.[49] These biases impede
people from remaining open to, or accepting, new ideas
or facts, even if they are true. Put simply: people listen
to arguments, gather information, and accept narratives
about life, in ways that confirm their pre-existing positions, especially when conflicting or contrary ideas or
stories threaten their group identity.[50]

If, for instance, people are told a particular piece of
information comes from a media outlet that harmonizes
with their political mega-group, they are more likely to
favor, and remain open to accepting, the information. The
opposite is also the case. Furthermore, when presented
with various perspectives related to a complex social
problem, people do not simply hear both perspectives and
weigh the evidence. Research indicates that *they do not
even hear* the other perspective. Writing on this subject,
Bill Bishop states: "Even if both sides of an issue are pre-

48. See Julie Schumacher Cohen, "In a Polarized World, Dialogue is a
    Radical Act," *America Magazine*, December 3, 2019, https://www.
    americamagazine.org/politics-society/2019/12/03/polarized-
    world-dialogue-radical-act.
49. Ian G. Anson, "Partisanship, Political Knowledge, and the Dunning-
    Kruger Effect," *Political Psychology* 39, no. 5 (2018): 1173–1192.
50. See Klein, *Why We're Polarized*, 81–102.

sented, people don't hear or don't remember arguments that counter their initial opinions."[51]

Other evidence of the 'closing' of the American mind flows from the existence of negative polarization, as was discussed in chapter two. Because of negative polarization, people are so appalled by their out-group interlocutor that, far from entertaining the ideas of an out-group member, they seek to destroy, shame, troll, or cancel people who offer diverging perspectives. In these cases, emotional rage, or feelings of fragility, impede people from remaining open to new or different perspectives.[52]

It is important to pause and note that few people will have the intellectual capacity of someone like Thomas Aquinas. Most people are not academics, and neither does everyone have the gifts or time needed to research, think abstractly, or read difficult treatises. What is more at stake, however, in the American situation, is that certain effects of polarization can impede a Christian's openness not just to intellectual ideas, but to people in general, including their stories, cultures, perspectives, feelings, and opinions. Rather than curiously engage the world around them, seeking wisdom and truth wherever they exist, polarization can direct one's mind to a limited investigation of the world.

In light of the importance of examining one's conscience in order to discern one's own spirit of 'catholicity,' the following questions might be helpful.

Does my Christian faith open me to the vast mysteries of the world, or have I become closed to different ideas, people, cultures, or experiences? Do I approach the world around me with fear and suspicion, or do I discern God's presence in creation?

---

51. Bishop, *The Big Sort*, 75.
52. See Lukianoff and Haidt, *The Coddling of the American.*

Do I make intentional decisions to read stories or listen to news outlets with which I tend to disagree, in order to hear a different perspective? Can I listen for common ground within that perspective? Do I read novels, seeking to gain the perspective of another, and to see the world from a different view? If I hold a position of leadership or authority, do I listen to all those I am called to serve so as to make decisions on their behalf?

Finally, when I engage in conversation with someone who holds different opinions, do I remain curious, ask clarifying questions, and discern their perspective? Can I remain respectful? Can I admit when I have been wrong, and thank another for introducing me to a new idea? Do I wait patiently with tension to allow the Holy Spirit to lead me, and my interlocutor, over time, to mutual understanding and truth?

Living with tension often means trying to reconcile one's Christian identity with the other identities in one's life. It is to this tension that I now turn.

Christians Growing in 'Apostolicity'

The Witness of Dorothy Day

For Christians to be 'apostolic' means, among other things, that they are to be more deeply rooted in, and thoroughly formed by, the tradition of faith that has been handed on to the Church by the apostles, such that they are able to live as witnesses to that tradition in the world. The founder of the Catholic Worker Movement, Dorothy Day (1897–1980), is a profound example in this regard.[53]

---

53. See Dorothy Day, *The Long Loneliness: The Autobiography of the Legendary Catholic Social Activist Dorothy Day* (New York: HarperOne,

A remarkable woman of her era, Day, throughout her entire life, investigated and, in many ways, appreciated and learned from different philosophies, ways of life, movements, and sources of culture. From a young age, she was a voracious and avid reader, a critical thinker, a tireless writer, and a lover of art. Her literary interests, time at university in Chicago, and life in New York City, put her in contact with bright, creative, and influential cultural icons and activists who shared her passions. She was also deeply political, wading in the waters of anarchism, communism, socialism, pacifism, and other political movements of her time. Most importantly, perhaps, people moved her, especially the poor; she listened to them, walked with them, was influenced by them, and, ultimately, dedicated her life to them, seeking, in many ways, to alleviate their plight.

Having roots in the Episcopal Church, she lived a life that was always haunted by God, even if faith took time to thoroughly influence her. As a young adult, she wrestled with the Christian tradition, and often rebelled against what she saw as a sclerotic and ineffectual Church. However, after being received into the Catholic Church in 1927, something slowly began to change within Day. She did not comprehensively reject the various influences that had informed her life, from people to political ideologies, and neither did she cease having questions about her faith or the role of the Church in the world. Rather, she slowly

1997). See, also, John Loughery and Blythe Randolph, *Dorothy Day: Dissenting Voice of the American Century* (New York: Simon and Schuster, 2020). See, also, Casey Cep, "Dorothy Day's Radical Faith: The Life and Legacy of the Catholic Writer and Activist, Who Some Hope will be Made a Saint," *The New Yorker*, April 6, 2020, https://www.newyorker.com/magazine/2020/04/13/dorothy-days-radical-faith.

chose to give herself, through prayer, worship, and discernment, preeminently to the tradition of the Church.

After becoming Catholic, she remained politically active, and never tired of serving the poor. However, whereas in her early years these areas of her life were influenced only tangentially by Christianity, and were far more influenced by political and philosophical ideologies, after her conversion, it was her faith that became her overarching guide. Living around many folks who did not share her views would, at times, make this difficult. However, she was consistent in allowing the gospel of Jesus Christ, including Jesus' invitation to serve the poor, along with the teaching authority of the Church, especially the tradition's social teaching, to saturate her soul.

This transformation was perplexing to those who knew Day prior to her entrance into the Catholic Church, to those with whom she remained politically active, and, especially to those who did not share her faith. Writing in her memoirs, she noted a conversation she had with a communist writer after her conversion. When asked how it was that she could believe what the Church taught, Day noted:

> I could only say that I believe in the Roman Catholic Church and all She teaches. I have accepted Her authority with my whole heart. At the same time I want to point out to you that we are taught to pray for final perseverance. We are taught that the gift of faith is a gift and sometimes I wonder why some have it and some do not. I feel my own unworthiness and can never be grateful enough to God for His gift of faith.[54]

---

54. See Dorothy Day, *From Union Square to Rome* (Silver Spring: Preservation, n.d.), online at https://www.catholicworker.org/dorothy-day/articles/212.pdf.

Day's commitment to her faith, and her openness to be informed by the tradition of the Church, even when she was questioned, critiqued, or pressured by others who did not share her faith, or when she herself had doubts, made her a bright light amid the poverty she encountered in the world. For these, and other reasons, she continues to shine as an example of what it means to live apostolicity in one's life.

A Struggle to Be Formed by Faith Today

To say that Christians today, in the United States, struggle to allow their identities to be thoroughly informed by their faith, that is, by the tradition that has been handed down through the apostles, would be an understatement.[55] On the one hand, there are, in increasing, unprecedented numbers, those who simply choose to walk away from Christianity, and who self-identify as 'unaffiliated.'[56] Of course, people leave Christianity for various reasons,[57]

---

55. Gloria Purvis, "Interview: Archbishop Cordileone on Biden, Pelosi, Abortion and Pope Francis," *America: The Jesuit Review*, November 9, 2021, https://www.americamagazine.org/faith/2021/11/09/archbishop-salvator-cordileone-gloria-purvis-podcast-241805. See, also, Ross Douthat, "The Shadow of Failure: A Reply to Edmund Waldstein," *First Things*, June 2022, https://www.firstthings.com/article/2022/06/the-shadow-of-failure.

56. David Masci and Gregory A. Smith, "7 Facts about American Catholics," *Pew Research Center*, October 10, 2018, https://www.pewresearch.org/fact-tank/2018/10/10/7-facts-about-american-catholics/. Pew Research Center, "In U.S., Decline of Christianity Continues at Rapid Pace," *Pew Research Center*, October 17, 2019, https://www.pewforum.org/2019/10/17/in-u-s-decline-of-christianity-continues-at-rapid-pace/. Brandon Vogt, "New Stats on Why Young People Leave the Church," *Brandon Vogt*, https://brandonvogt.com/new-stats-young-people-leave-church/.

57. Vogt, "New Stats."

and not everyone does so simply because they do not want the Christian vision to inform their lives. Many in the Church have left, not necessarily because they do not find the gospel of Jesus convincing, but because of scandals or grievances they have experienced within the Church.[58]

On the other hand, other identities in people's lives, particularly their political identity, replace or diminish their commitment to Christianity. The reality of political mega-identities, as was explored in chapter two, means that politics, in the American context, influences most every area of people's lives, and sometimes in an exaggerated way. One consequence of this is that some Christians listen to political leaders and parties for guidance in their lives of faith—and in many other areas of their lives—even though those same political leaders and parties do not necessarily have the expertise, or the credibility, to do so.[59] Sometimes they (the political leaders) even speak and act in ways that can be misleading regarding important moral and social questions about which the Church's tradition has much to say. Another consequence is that, in other instances, Christians are influenced by their own Christian leaders who have become intoxicated by political ideologies that undermine the Christian vision.[60] The ris-

---

58. On this point, see Elizabeth Tenety, "Not Right or Left, Wrong or Right: Millennial Catholics and the Age of Mercy," in *Polarization in the US Catholic Church*, 113–118.

59. See Jeffrey Salkin, "President Trump is a Religious Leader," *Religion News*, November 17, 2020, https://religionnews.com/2020/11/17/trump-election/. See, also, George Weigel, "'Matthew 25 Catholics'?" *First Things*, August 17, 2022, https://www.firstthings.com/web-exclusives/2022/08/matthew-25-catholics.

60. See Tim Alberta, "How Politics Poisoned the Evangelical Church," *The Atlantic*, May 10, 2022, https://www.theatlantic.com/magazine/archive/2022/06/evangelical-church-pastors-political-radicalization/629631/.

ing influence of politics in people's lives, in ways that contradict Christian faith, can be seen in statistical research.

For instance, a recent Pew Research report notes that when "it comes to specific policy issues, Catholics are often more aligned with their political party than with the teachings of their church."[61] On the issue of abortion, for example, 77 percent of Catholics who self-identify as Democrat or are Democratic-leaning think abortion should be legal in all or most cases. 36 percent of Republicans or Republican-leaning adults think similarly. When considering Catholics overall, the percentage is 56.[62] When it comes to whether same-sex couples should be allowed to marry, 59 percent of Catholic Republicans respond favorably while 76 percent of Catholic Democrats feel the same.[63] These statistics are illuminating, especially given the Church's clear and fairly consistent teaching regarding the legalization of abortion and same-sex marriage.[64]

---

61. Gregory A. Smith, "8 Facts about Catholics and Politics in the U.S.," *Pew Research Center*, September 15, 2020, https://www.pewresearch.org/fact-tank/2020/09/15/8-facts-about-catholics-and-politics-in-the-u-s/.

62. See Pew Research Center, "Fact Sheet: Public Opinion on Abortion," *Pew Research Center*, May 17, 2022, https://www.pewresearch.org/religion/fact-sheet/public-opinion-on-abortion/.

63. Michael Lipka and Gregory A. Smith, "Like Americans Overall, U.S. Catholics are Sharply Divided by Party," *Pew Research Center*, January 24, 2019, https://www.pewresearch.org/fact-tank/2019/01/24/like-americans-overall-u-s-catholics-are-sharply-divided-by-party/.

64. On this point, see a helpful array of resources found on these sites: https://www.usccb.org/committees/laity-marriage-family-life-youth/same-sex-unions; https://www.usccb.org/issues-and-action/human-life-and-dignity/abortion/on-the-prochoice-position-on-abortion. See, also, United States Conferences of Catholic Bishops, *Marriage: Love and Life in the Divine Plan: A Pastoral Letter of the United States Conference of Catholic Bishops*, November 17, 2009, https://www.usccb.org/resources/pastoral-letter-marriage-love-and-life-in-the-divine-plan.pdf.

Again, statistics often do not capture the nuance of any one person's position. And it is beyond the purpose of this book to debate the finer points of these issues. Conversation and dialogue around these important themes would likely reveal the intricate relationship between faith and politics in the lives of many Catholics (and other Christians). These conversations should be entertained, especially in divided times.[65]

Nevertheless, another indication that the Catholic living tradition is not a thoroughly influential source for Catholics is found in statistics regarding faith practices.[66] For example, 47 percent of conservative Catholics said they seldom or never read scripture, while 58 percent of liberal Catholics said the same. Religion was also not indicated as being very influential in forming either conservative or liberal Catholic perspectives on morality. Only 40 percent of conservatives cited religion as a source of guidance, and 25 percent of liberals said the same.

Not considering religion as a source of morality is a far cry from the witness of Dorothy Day, who sought intentionally to align her political and moral views with the insights given to her by Jesus Christ and the Church, and who strengthened her political commitments and service to the poor through an active life of prayer and worship. Given the challenges posed by the polarization of American

---

65. See Peter Coleman, "On Abortion, Now is the Time to Talk," *Divided We Fall*, June 24, 2022, https://dividedwefall.org/on-abortion-now-is-the-time-to-talk/.

66. Pew Research Center, "Religious Landscape Study: Political Ideology among Catholics," *Pew Research Center*, https://www.pewforum.org/religious-landscape-study/religious-tradition/catholic/political-ideology/. For more on the possible consequences of the challenges related to Christian identity, see Ross Douthat, "A Gentler Christendom," *First Things*, June 2022, https://www.firstthings.com/article/2022/06/a-gentler-christendom.

society regarding the ability of Christians to cultivate apostolicity in their lives, that is, to allow the robust tradition of the Church to be the preeminent source of influence in their lives, the following questions may be helpful.

Does my relationship with Jesus, and the tradition given to me through the scriptures, along with the teachings of the Church, inform my life more than the political party to which I belong? If my friends were asked what identity was most important to me, how would they answer? Is my belief in Jesus known to others? Do I let my partisan preferences impede my ability to live the Christian faith? If so, what does this look like?

During election cycles, do I revisit the Church's guidance for participating in democratic elections?[67] Have I considered the words of different ecclesial leaders concerning how to cultivate a better kind of politics?[68] Have I taken time to read through the social teaching of the Church? Does this social teaching inform my decisions, and does it invite me to challenge the platform of the political party to which I belong?

What are the various ways I practice my faith? Do I spend quality time with my family and friends praying and worshipping? How does the practice of my faith influence my political decisions?[69] Am I willing to place the worship of Jesus at the center of my life and avoid political idols,

---

67. See https://www.usccb.org/offices/justice-peace-human-development/forming-consciences-faithful-citizenship for more information.

68. On this point, see, for instance, Pope Francis, *Fratelli Tutti*, October 3, 2020, https://www.vatican.va/content/francesco/en/encyclicals/documents/papa-francesco_20201003_enciclica-fratelli-tutti.html.

69. See, for instance, Mark P. Shea, *The Church's Best-Kept Secret: A Primer on Catholic Social Teaching* (Hyde Park: New City Press, 2020).

especially political leaders who claim to represent the Christian tradition, or worse, pursue messiah-like status?

Conclusion

Now that the marks of the Church have been explored with an eye to the way in which polarized culture can affect Christian living, I am going to look at one particular response Christians have made to the culture of polarization, which has resulted in many negative consequences. With an eye toward the Author of the hope that surpasses all understanding, a possible solution will be explored.

Chapter Four

Responding to the Storms of Polarization

"They are doing *what?*"

After gathering supplies to prepare for the arrival of Hurricane Florence, and having safeguarded my house from high winds and copious rain, I settled into a somewhat unhealthy routine of frantically tracking the hurricane's movement on my phone. I was addicted to my phone's information—even more than usual—and I craved the latest hurricane update.

Noticing that my behavior was less than healthy (I think I was developing a facial tic), and having grown tired of the weather app, I changed tactics and pulled up my search engine. Typing in Florence revealed many hits, one that I couldn't believe: a Facebook page inviting people to shoot their guns at the hurricane to 'scare' it away.[1]

Wait. Hold on. They are doing *what?*

---

1. See the following site for more information on this topic: https://archive.ph/4zLKg.

Incredulous that people would actually attempt this, the next article's title was even more shocking: "Myrtle Beach Man Who Shot at Hurricane Florence Dies After Bullet Ricochets."[2]

Have people lost their minds? This cannot be true, I thought to myself.

As 'fact checking' the Internet had become commonplace during those days when stories about the possibility of 'fake news' flooded headlines, I sought more information before sharing the link with my family. Thankfully, after a little research, it was clear that the story of the man's death was fictitious. And the Facebook page was merely a joke. It contained the following disclaimer: "Note: do not actually discharge firearms into the air. You could kill someone and you cannot frighten a hurricane. I cant [sic] believe I actually have to write this." Indeed, I could not believe it as well.

My fact-checking pursuits revealed, however—in a manner highlighting humanity's unwavering ability to make something worse out of an already dangerous situation—that in previous hurricanes, such as Irma in 2017, people were already being invited to shoot at hurricanes,[3] were taking this seriously, and needed to be reminded that going Al Pacino in Scarface on a storm comprised of winds swirling over 180 miles per hour could easily put oneself and others, in danger.[4] When confronted by the terror of

---

2.   See Amanda Hamilton, "Myrtle Beach Man Who Shot At Hurricane Florence Dies After Bullet Ricochets," *CGC News*, September 13, 2018, https://archive.ph/uDcUo. This story was determined to be false. See Dan Mac Guill, "Did a Man Die from Shooting a Gun at Hurricane Florence?" *Snopes*, September 14, 2018, https://www.snopes.com/fact-check/myrtle-beach-shooting-gun-hurricane-florence/.

3.   For more information on this topic, see https://archive.ph/LsTnv.

4.   See Associated Press, "Florida Man's Joke About Shooting Irma Gets Taken Seriously," September 10, 2017, https://www.snopes.com/

hurricanes, it was evident that people could be tempted to respond in any number of ways, some helpful, and others downright dangerous.

As the storms of polarized groups have formed in the United States, many people, including members of the Church, have employed various responses to meet the challenges. More than a few have been beneficial and will be explored in more detail in subsequent chapters. Others, however, mirroring the disastrous idea of unloading lead bullets into a tempest, do not seem to have improved the situation. In fact, these attempts likely have made matters worse, intensifying division between different groups, increasing feelings of anger and hostility, and undermining the witness that Christians are to provide to the world through their missionary efforts.

What follows in this chapter is an exploration of one particular response Christians have utilized in their missionary efforts to engage the challenges of polarization: approaching polarization through the lens of the 'culture war.'

To navigate this exploration, I will survey the emergence of the culture war in the American context over the last few decades, indicate how this has been tied to the life and mission of the Church, and show why this response is problematic for Christians who desire to engage the world in polarized times. Both to highlight the limitations inherent in utilizing war as a metaphor for the mission of the Church, and to begin to explore how the Church might engage the challenge of polarization through a

---

ap/2017/09/10/florida-mans-joke-shooting-irma-gets-taken-seriously/. See, also, Michael Edison Hayden, "Sheriff Warns Against People 'Shooting' Hurricane Irma," ABC News, September 10, 2017, https://abcnews.go.com/US/sheriff-warns-people-shooting-hurricane-irma/story?id=49741491.

Christ-centered and Christ-influenced approach, I will appropriate the wisdom of the early Church, especially that provided in Paul's letter to the Philippians. From this tradition, I will propose that Christ's incarnational movement is the metaphor that Christians should use in order to engage the hurricanes of polarization darkening the American skies.

Some Preliminary Points

Before beginning my analysis of the inherent problems existing when the Church uses the metaphor of war to respond to polarized times, I want to make a few preliminary observations.

First, the culture war has a complex history in the United States involving both political parties, left and right.[5] Since my concern in this chapter is the way in which Christians have been affected by recourse to the culture war metaphor, and since most Christians statistically align with the Republican Party, I will necessarily need to focus specifically on the GOP. This is not done to throw support behind a particular partisan side. Again, throughout this book, I have assiduously attempted not to be partisan. Rather, my choice for focusing on the conservative mega-group is fitting, as the war metaphor has been particularly influential in the Republican Party over the last four decades, and this influence has affected the

---

5. See, for instance, Hartman, *A War for the Soul*. See, also, James Davison Hunter, *Culture Wars: The Struggle to Define America* (New York: Basic Books, 1991). See, also, Thomas B. Edsall, "'Lean Into It. Lean Into the Culture War.'" *The New York Times*, July 14, 2021, https://www.nytimes.com/2021/07/14/opinion/culture-war-democrats-republicans.html?searchResultPosition=7.

imagination of many Christians by way of their association with the conservative mega-group.[6]

Furthermore, and to my second preliminary point, I am not overly concerned in this text with the political debates around, or the political ramifications of, the culture wars, even though these political considerations intersect with the purpose of this chapter. Rather, I am interested in exploring how the pervasive presence of the culture war metaphor affects Christian missionary discipleship, i.e., the thoughts and actions of Christians who engage in the world, regardless of whether this engagement is explicitly ecclesial in nature. This point deserves some explanation.

As has been made clear in this book, I maintain that, if one is a Christian, one's identity *as a Christian* should be the preeminent identity in a person's life, and that missionary discipleship is, therefore, the primary task of any Christian. This is the case whether a Christian is engaged in explicitly ecclesial activities, such as teaching religious education, praying for a member of her parish, or attending worship, or whether she is engaged in less-obviously ecclesial activities, such as casting a vote, or working at a food pantry, which nevertheless require the guidance of the vision given by Christ and the Christian tradition. In other words, Christians, if they desire to live the demands of the gospel, cannot compartmentalize their faith, maintaining their relationship with Christ and the consequences that flow from this relationship in some situations, while ignoring the ramifications of that relationship in others. It is this relationship with Christ, along with the missionary imperative that flows from this relation-

---

6.   See Steve Kornacki, *The Red and the Blue: The 1990s and the Birth of Political Tribalism* (New York: HarperCollins, 2018), 1-44. See, also, Robert Wuthnow, *Christianity in the 21st Century: Reflections on the Challenges Ahead* (New York: Oxford University Press, 1993). See, also, French, *Divided We Fall*.

ship, and how the utilization of a war metaphor affects both, that is my concern in this chapter.

Finally, using 'war' as a metaphor as Christians engage in the task of evangelization is not the only problematic response that Christians and others have utilized in polarized times. 'Cancel culture,' where, among other things, people suppress or 'cancel' either public expression of, or the people who espouse, certain ideas, rather than engage with these perspectives or people, is a challenge in the American context that appears to be intensifying the problem of polarization.[7] Greg Lukianoff and Jonathan Haidt, arguably experts on this and related themes, conclude in their book *The Coddling of the American Mind*, that this type of culture (they refer to it as 'call-out culture') displays a *"vindictive protectiveness"* that undermines people's ability to "practice the essential skills of critical thinking and civil disagreement."[8] Even as 'cancel culture' remains an unfortunate response in polarizing times, this challenge has been addressed in a thorough and generally convincing way in Lukianoff and Haidt's work, as well as in other research.[9] Therefore, I will forego further analysis of this theme. To my knowledge, however, the damage the war metaphor has caused to Christian discipleship and mission has not been comprehensively explored in reference to polarization.[10]

It is to this theme that I now turn.

---

7. See Stanley, *Not in It to Win It*, 35–58.
8. See *The Coddling of the American*, 10–11.
9. See French, *Divided We Fall*, 101–116. See, also, Lukianoff and Haidt, *The Coddling of the American*. See, also, Jonathan Rauch, *The Constitution of Knowledge: A Defense of Truth* (Washington, DC: Brookings Institutional Press, 2021).
10. For a recent article on the culture war and Catholic ethics, see M. Therese Lysaught, "Reclaiming the Catholic Moral and Intellectual Tradition from the Culture Wars," *National Catholic Reporter*, April 7, 2022, https://www.ncronline.org/news/opinion/reclaiming-catholic-moral-and-intellectual-tradition-culture-wars.

The Culture War: In Their Own Words

There is a long and complex history of the rise of the culture war in the American context, along with the utilization of war as a metaphor to guide political and religious engagement within the culture of the United States. A reasonable starting place for a brief analysis of this reality is the Republican Party of the 1980s under the influential rhetoric and leadership of Newt Gingrich.

In his book *The Red and the Blue: The 1990s and the Birth of Political Tribalism*, Steve Kornacki documents how Gingrich, in the early 1980s, as a newly elected Republican Congressman of Georgia, transformed the Republican Party's influence and identity in the House of Representatives.[11] Republicans, facing, at that time, a dominant Democratic stronghold in the House spanning decades, were led by Gingrich from being a silent and somewhat ineffectual minority, to being a bold, evocative, and challenging thorn in the side of the Democratic majority under the leadership of Tip O'Neill (1912–1994).[12] Through shrewd use of televised hearings, antagonistic and atypical hostile procedures on the House floor, and intensified rhetoric—including somewhat unprecedented insults for the time leveled at members of the other party—Gingrich laid the foundation for a more combative Republican Party.[13] In his own words, he stated: "I think

11. See Kornacki, *The Red and the Blue*, especially 27–44. See, also, Jonathan Haidt, "Why the Past 10 Years of American Life Have Been Uniquely Stupid: It's Not Just a Phase," *The Atlantic*, April 11, 2022, https://www.theatlantic.com/magazine/archive/2022/05/social-media-democracy-trust-babel/629369/.

12. See Edsall, "'Lean Into It.'"

13. See Kornacki, *The Red and the Blue*, 27–44. See Haidt, "Why the Past."

you're going to see a much tougher and a much more militant Republican Party."[14] He was prophetic in this regard.

Fast forward to 1992. Standing before the Republican National Convention, Patrick Buchanan, a practicing Catholic, in a speech laced with references to America's history of armed conflict, was quite blatant in his appropriation of war as a metaphor to guide political and, what is more, *religious* engagement in the American context. He stated: "There is a religious war going on in this country. It is a cultural war...for the soul of America." Amid the rapt attention of many, Buchanan stressed: This culture war is as "critical to the kind of nation we shall be as was the Cold War itself..."[15] Indicating how high were the stakes for Republicans in general, and for religious believers, in particular, Buchanan ratcheted up the intensity as he continued: The outcome of this cultural war would decide "who we [Americans] are," "what we believe," and whether the "Judeo-Christian values and beliefs upon which this nation was built" would remain influentially dominant in the United States.

What emerged on the floor of the House in the 1980s under Gingrich was becoming the prevailing paradigm, as seen in Buchanan's speech, for engaging the so-called political and religious 'other': war and enmity for the very salvation of America.

It is important to pause and note the conceptual transition that was taking place, along with some of the consequences laden within, the rhetoric emerging between the

---

14. Kornacki, *The Red and the Blue*, 44.
15. See Hartman, *A War for the Soul*, 1. See, also, Patrick Joseph Buchanan, "Culture War Speech: Address to the Republican National Convention," *Voices of Democracy: The U.S. Oratory Project*, https://voicesofdemocracy.umd.edu/buchanan-culture-war-speech-speech-text/.

1980s and 1990s in conservative circles. Gingrich's rhetoric was primarily, though not exclusively, a political call to arms within the Republican Party, inviting Republicans to a more combative position within the party itself, and directed toward those men and women sitting across the aisle in Congress. By the 1990s, however, political *and* religious concerns were interwoven quite seamlessly through the utilization of war as a metaphor. For the uncritical listener exposed to the voices of many conservatives, Republicans were aligning themselves almost exclusively with conservative Christians for a theo-political battle against a clearly demarcated enemy: Democrats, non-believers, and so-called non-conservative, or theologically liberal, Christians. This enemy—*even though their rank included many who were actually Christians*—was likened to atheistic Communists whose finger was still close to the red button that could bring about the destruction of all that was valuable in America.

What is more, it was significant that not only was it posited by the increasingly militant right that political policy and power were at stake in the culture war. But, more urgently, as Buchanan emphasized, what was now at stake was the very salvation of America, a theme that could not be more saturated with Christian theological language. This salvation could only be guaranteed, it was suggested, not through Jesus Christ and the grace of his Church (even though, to be fair, this was likely important to many involved), but through members of the Republican Party engaging in, and winning, the political-religious culture war. This 'eschatological' fervor guaranteed to enshrine the mentality that each subsequent election cycle was 'the most important election ever,' not just for one's party, but, even more, for the very soul of America.

As the 90s gave way to a new millennium, the utilization of the war metaphor would not disappear.

In 2007, David French, a conservative evangelical who, only in the age of Trump, rejected his affiliation with the Republican Party, gave a speech at a conservative conference where he transformed the war metaphor in light of the tenor of the times. In comments he would come to regret, he would liken those on the left to none other than the kinds of terrorists who took down the World Trade Center towers, and committed other heinous acts, thereby taking the lives of thousands of innocent Americans. French stated: "I believe the two greatest threats to America are university leftism at home and jihadism abroad, and I feel called to fight both."[16] In light of 1) the terrorist attacks on that tragic day in September, 2) two major wars against terrorism in which the United States was embroiled whose death counts continued to rise, and 3) revelations from Guantanamo Bay of the tactics used by Americans against some terrorists held as prisoners, few more damning, and evocatively militaristic, words could have been chosen to express one's disdain for—and allude to the possibility of unfettered tactics to be used against—members of another political party.[17]

Only after being engaged in a real war in Iraq as a JAG officer, and witnessing some of the horrors of actual war, would French return to the United States and realize the

---

16. French, *Divided We Fall*, 6.
17. This sad trend would continue leading up to the 2016 Presidential election. An article by Michael Anton, written under the pseudonym of Publius Decius Mus, entitled "The Flight 93 Election," utilized similar metaphorical references equating out-group members with terrorists. See Publius Decius Mus, "The Flight 93 Election: The Election of 2016 Will Test Whether Virtù Remains in the Core of the American Nation," *Claremont Review of Books*, September 5, 2016, https://claremontreviewofbooks.com/digital/the-flight-93-election/.

folly of his words and actions. He would state: "My time in Iraq had changed me. It had also educated me. It changed my regard for my fellow citizens, especially my political opponents. If I had been willing to die for them while wearing the uniform of my country, why should I regard them as mortal enemies today? Wrong on the law and on policy, yes. But a threat to the country in the way I'd framed them before I went to war? No."[18] Suggestive of one who had gone through a conversion of sorts, French, in reference to his war allusions, stated: "I'm ashamed of those words."[19]

No sooner had French had a change of heart regarding the appropriateness of the war metaphor, however, did he find himself on the opposite side of the battle, where he was now viewed by some conservatives as the very enemy that required defeat.

In 2019, an internecine conservative debate ignited. Catholic convert and conservative political journalist Sohrab Ahmari had grown weary of what he perceived was the approach of French and others to the challenges facing conservatives in the American context.[20] In the face of his disillusionment, the former Op-Ed editor of the *New York Post* unflinchingly embraced war as a metaphor to form his critique against David French.

According to Ahmari, French, on account of his comments and stated political philosophy, had capitulated

18. French, *Divided We Fall*, 9.

19. French, *Divided We Fall*, 6.

20. For a few articles in reference to French's position, see David French, "A *New York Times* Op-Ed is Very Wrong About Religious Liberty," *National Review*, May 7, 2019, https://www.nationalreview.com/corner/new-york-times-wrong-religious-liberty/. See, also, Benjamin Wallace-Wells, "David French, Sohrab Ahmari, and the Battle for the Future of Conservatism," *The New Yorker*, September 12, 2019, https://www.newyorker.com/news/the-political-scene/david-french-sohrab-ahmari-and-the-battle-for-the-future-of-conservatism.

to the so-called progressive enemy.[21] French needed to recognize that there was a "crisis facing religious conservatives."[22] The only response, *á la* Ahmari, was "to fight the culture war with the aim of defeating the enemy and enjoying the spoils in the form of a public square re-ordered to the common good and ultimately the Highest Good." For Ahmari, positioning himself against not only progressives, but now seemingly against French-style classically liberal Republicans, "war and enmity" were necessary themes to employ on account of tactics used by the so-called enemy. This response was not just a political move. It was a decidedly Christian tactic, in contradistinction to French's "different Christian strategy." As both men were publicly committed to their Christian faith, Ahmari's invective against French showed that it was now unapologetically acceptable to some to use war as a lens to view interactions not just between two different political parties, but between members of the same Body of Christ.

Though Ahmari and French would proceed to debate together in various fora around this topic and clarify some of their differences in ways slightly more becoming of fellow members of the Body of Christ, the damage had been done.[23] New 'battle lines' had been drawn, new enemies defined, and similar militaristic rhetoric employed, now glossed with the shine of being an explicitly missional 'Christian strategy.' What began as metaphorical bullets shot into the polarized hurricane of an oppositional mega-group were now being directed at those once holding the weapons within one's own hurricane. Things were heating

21. See Sohrab Ahmari, "Against David French-ism," *First Things*, May 29, 2019, https://www.firstthings.com/web-exclusives/2019/05/against-david-french-ism.

22. For the following quotes, see Ahmari, "Against David."

23. See Wallace-Wells, "David French."

up between, and within, the polarized hurricanes of the American context.

In closing out this section, I want to highlight that the utilization of the culture war metaphor is now ubiquitous across the political and theological spectrum, both on the right *and on the left*.[24] Even as I write, new headlines and articles emerge pulling on this metaphor.[25] Wajahat Ali of *The Daily Beast*, for instance, invites Democrats to "bring brass knuckles to the knife fight [with conservatives]", "take out Republican's knees", and "fully engage in the culture war."[26] This example and others indicate that the 'war metaphor' has become common parlance, nearly unavoidable for mainstream authors, journalists, and theologians,

---

24. Frank Bruni, "Republicans Have Found Their Cruel New Culture War," *The New York Times*, April 10, 2021, https://www.nytimes.com/2021/04/10/opinion/sunday/transgender-rights-republicans-arkansas.html?searchResultPosition=8. See, also, Sarah Mervosh and Giulia Heyward, "Schools are Caught in the Cross Hairs of America's Culture Wars," *The New York Times*, August 18, 2021, https://www.nytimes.com/2021/08/18/world/schools-are-caught-in-the-cross-hairs-of-americas-culture-wars.html?searchResultPosition=14. Tom Deignan, "In an Age of Insurrections and Culture Wars, Joyce and Faulkner are Increasingly Relevant," *American Magazine*, March 31, 2022, https://www.americamagazine.org/arts-culture/2022/03/31/joyce-faulkner-gunmen-politics-242706. Zach Stanton, "How the 'Culture War' Could Break Democracy," *Politico*, May 20, 2021, https://www.politico.com/news/magazine/2021/05/20/culture-war-politics-2021-democracy-analysis-489900. Alexander Stern, "Benjamin's Warning: When Politics is an Exercise in Style, Democracy Suffers," *Commonweal Magazine*, November 29, 2021, https://www.commonwealmagazine.org/benjamins-warning.

25. Jamelle Bouie, "Democrats, You Can't Ignore the Culture Wars Any Longer," *The New York Times*, April 22, 2022, https://www.nytimes.com/2022/04/22/opinion/red-scare-culture-wars.html.

26. See Wajahat Ali, "If Dems Fought an All-Out Culture War, They'd Win," *The Daily Beast*, August 5, 2022, https://www.thedailybeast.com/if-democrats-fought-an-all-out-culture-war-against-republicans-theyd-win?ref=scroll.

and affecting, even if somewhat unconsciously, nearly all Christians and partisans in the United States. With its ubiquity, why should usage of this metaphor be questioned by Christians (and others) as they seek to understand, and respond to, the challenges posed by polarization in general and, more importantly, to their call to be missionary disciples, in particular? The answer to this question lies in the intoxicating, oftentimes indirect, influence that metaphors have on framing and forming human understanding of, and action in, the world—and how devastating this can be for Christian discipleship when war is a metaphor that Christians live by.

The Power of Metaphors

To understand the effect the utilization of war as a metaphor can have on Christian identity, it is important to analyze the nature of metaphors—that is, what role metaphors play in people's daily lives, and how they inform human beings. A helpful starting place for this analysis is the work of two linguists and philosophers, George Lakoff and Mark Johnson.

In their 1980 classic *Metaphors We Live By*, Lakoff and Johnson draw several conclusions regarding metaphors, three of which are germane to this chapter.

First, metaphors are unavoidable, and serve more than a rhetorical function. They influence how human beings relate to, understand, and act in the world. As Lakoff and Johnson state: "We have found...that metaphor is pervasive in everyday life, not just in language but in thought and action. Our ordinary conceptual system, in terms of which we both think and act, is fundamentally metaphorical in nature."[27] This means that the metaphors people live by, existing both in speech and in thought, are doing more than serving people's ability to communicate. They are forming, at a fundamental level, how people understand and relate to the world around them.[28]

A brief example can be helpful.

If the primary metaphor I use in reference to my job is that it is a nightmare, I will likely do more than just use language related to a nightmare to refer to my work. The negative connotations related to a 'nightmare' will likely influence my thoughts and actions in reference to my workplace environment. As one usually does not desire to remain in a nightmare for too long, I may seek to terminate my job and find other possibilities—perhaps doing so somewhat hastily—in order to escape the nightmare. Still more, as a nightmare, I am not likely to consider any possible benefits of my employment. (Only the bravest person seeks a silver lining in a nightmare.) It might be, for instance, a challenge for me to see positive opportunities that present themselves within my work environment, or it might be difficult for me to stand in solidarity with co-workers who may need my encouragement to endure the workplace environment. These co-workers could be a possible way to improve the nightmarish workplace, but I could be impeded from seeing this opportunity, because my co-workers may be (falsely) understood as ghoulish characters in a terrible dream.

---

27. George Lakoff and Mark Johnson, *Metaphors We Live By* (Chicago: The University of Chicago Press, 2003), 3.
28. For the way in which metaphors can influence how scientists approach their fields of research, see George Zarkadakis, *In Our Own Image: Savior or Destroyer? The History and Future of Artificial Intelligence* (New York and London: Pegasus Books, 2015).

The second point that Lakoff and Johnson highlight regarding metaphors is that they can influence thought and action indirectly or even unconsciously.[29] When people use metaphors in their language, or within their thought processes, they may not always be aware of the multitudinous ways that a metaphor is shaping their thoughts and actions, or their overall understanding of reality. Referring to the example above, I can depict my job as a nightmare without explicitly realizing that doing so raises my anxiety every Sunday evening as I prepare to return to work. I may be vegging out and watching football and notice myself becoming anxious for no apparent reason. The power of the nightmarish connotations related to my work can creep into my thoughts and imagination and induce stress, even if I am not consciously bringing this metaphor to mind, or directly analyzing how this metaphor is affecting me.

Finally, Lakoff and Johnson note that metaphors are simultaneously illuminating and distorting. Since a metaphor shows a relationship between one thing and another, and since the two things brought into a relationship by the metaphor are not identical, there will be ways that a metaphor accurately highlights aspects of that to which it refers, and ways in which the metaphor misses the mark, so to speak. As the linguists note:

> The very systematicity that allows us to comprehend one aspect of a concept in terms of another... will necessarily hide other aspects of the concept. In allowing us to focus on one aspect of a concept...a metaphorical concept can keep us from focusing on other aspects of the concept that are inconsistent with that metaphor.[30]

---

29. Lakoff and Johnson, *Metaphors We Live By*, 3.
30. Lakoff and Johnson, *Metaphors We Live By*, 10.

This part of the theory of metaphors can seem somewhat abstract and convoluted. However, the main point is that metaphors can be useful in accurately depicting, or 'highlighting,' something about the world around human beings, but they can also do so inaccurately, 'hiding' something equally true about the nature of reality.

Lakoff and Johnson's insights that metaphors 'hide' and 'highlight' can illuminate the challenges inherent in the culture war metaphor.

War as a Metaphor and the Demands of the Gospel

Before applying Lakoff and Johnson's insights to an analysis of the war metaphor, it is important to delimit the scope of this section. I am only concerned with the relationship between the war metaphor and *Christian mission*. To be clear, what follows is not a philosophical conversation about the necessity of war or self-defense in general, or a discussion concerning 'just war,' in particular. I am chiefly interested in the metaphorical value of war in relationship to mission, i.e., the way in which the utilization of war as a metaphor informs Christians who seek to live their ecclesial relationship with Jesus and make present the message of the gospel in the world around them.

So how can or does the war metaphor inform Christian mission? To answer this question, three basic contours concerning mission[31] need to be considered: that which

31. It is important to point out that the way I am using the term 'mission' will be explored throughout the remainder of this chapter, and the rest of the book. However, 'mission,' should not be confused with 'proselytism.' The latter, in contradistinction to the former, involves methods of proclaiming the gospel that do not respect the inherent

motivates Christians to engage in mission; how Christians understand the *other* whom they are engaging in their mission; and what this missionary *engagement* involves. These three contours of mission theology will guide the following investigation.[32]

A Charitable Assessment of the War Metaphor

To begin, it is necessary to give a charitable assessment of the war metaphor in relationship to Christian mission. Clearly, I will be arguing that this metaphor impedes Christians from living the demands of the gospel, and I will be using much of the remainder of this chapter to debate this point. Nevertheless, there are ways that the war metaphor, at least tangentially, 'highlights' true aspects of Christian mission. This is perhaps why it is such an enticing, though still misleading, metaphor to utilize.

On the one hand, the war metaphor stresses a sense of urgency for engagement and, in doing so, *motivates* people to act. In some circumstances, war arises because what people value, cherish, and love, is being threatened. There is something at stake, something that can be lost, or something that requires preservation: whether this is one's land, family, home, beliefs, or one's own life. If war is imminent or already initiated, people will be motivated, or perhaps even forced, to act.

---

dignity of each person, nor the person's free assent to the truth.

32. On these themes of mission, see Robert Aaron Wessman, *Missionary Options for a Secular Age: Remaining in the World for the Salvation of the World* (Leuven: Unpublished Dissertation, 2019), https://researchportal.be/en/publication/missionary-options-secular-age-remaining-world-salvation-world.

Indeed, there is, to a certain extent, an urgency that should be felt by—i.e., should be motivating—all Christians to engage in mission. Jesus' command to his disciples in this regard is straightforward: "Go," he exhorts, and engage in mission (Mt. 28:16-20)! "Salvation is at stake," he reminds his followers, and there are impediments in the world to salvation (cf. Acts 1:7-8; Mt. 10:16). If Christians do not act in accord with their missionary calling, there can be eternal consequences (Mt. 25:31-46). Members of the Body of Christ, therefore, are to be concerned that their own family, friends, and the entire world, can receive and live the message of the gospel and participate in integral salvation—which is the fullness of life that can only come through Christ and the Church (Jn. 10:10). Ultimately, mission is so crucial that it is deemed essential to the very life of the Church.[33]

The war metaphor motivates people to act, and a Christian's concern for mission ought to do the same.

On the other hand, the sacrificial nature of war—that people lay down their lives for others when engaging in war—speaks to a reality inherent in Christian mission. Fighting in a war often requires people to place their own life in harm's way, and to set aside immediate needs for a greater good.[34] Engagement in war often requires postponement of gratification, which includes a willingness to sacrifice in the moment so that a future realization of what one desires for one's family, country, or even oneself, can

---

33. See David J. Bosch, *Transforming Mission: Paradigm Shifts in the Theology of Mission* (Maryknoll: Orbis Books, 2014); see, also, Bevans and Schroeder, *Constants in Context*.

34. See Tim Kennedy and Nick Palmisciano, *Scars and Stripes: An Unapologetically American Story of Fighting the Taliban, UFC Warriors, and Myself* (New York: Atria Books, 2022).

be possible.[35] These notes of war resonate with aspects of Christianity.

For instance, being a disciple of Jesus Christ requires sacrifice. As Christian author and literary critic G.K. Chesterton (1874–1936) rightly noted: "The Christian ideal has not been tried and found wanting. It has been found difficult; and left untried."[36] Jesus' words are clear that the greatest act of love is to sacrifice—that is, to lay down—one's life for another (Jn. 15:13). As Jesus serves, and sacrifices for, his disciples, he invites them to do the same for others (Jn. 13). Carrying one's cross, as Jesus did toward his death on Calvary, is a distinct marker of discipleship (Mt. 16:24-28). This is why, from the beginning of Christianity, martyrdom, that is, dying for the sake of one's faith and the promulgation of the gospel—i.e., dying for the sake of the Church's mission—has been sought as an ideal.

That sacrifice is involved in war *and* in mission does indicate, therefore, another kind of relationship between the two.

But this is where the metaphor begins to fail.

The War Metaphor and the 'Other'

Take, for example, the way that war defines the other as an enemy, and what this can entail when applied to Christian mission.

In war, the 'other' is almost always posited as a clearly defined enemy, with little room for distinctions, variations,

---

35. See Jordan B. Peterson, *12 Rules for Life: An Antidote to Chaos* (Canada: Random House, 2018), 31–66; 161–202.
36. See G.K. Chesterton, *What's Wrong with the World* (Project Gutenberg, 2008), https://www.gutenberg.org/files/1717/1717-h/1717-h.htm.

or nuances, in which, often, great efforts are made to reduce the other to something 'less than human,' or lacking dignity.[37] Warriors do not ordinarily sit around discussing the finer points of the enemy's perspective, or the ways in which their enemy quite possibly has much in common with them. This would make their task of destroying the enemy far too difficult.

One recalls here the surprise that came to German and British troops during World War I when, on Christmas, fighting ceased, and warriors on opposing sides, *who were minutes earlier killing each other*, found themselves singing hymns together as fellow Christians in honor of Jesus Christ's birth.[38] The commonalities between enemies do not have to be as profound as sharing the same religion: simply recognizing that one's enemy has a family to return to, and most likely would rather be home than fighting and killing other human beings, are the nuances of one's enemy that, in war, are not often recognized. Indeed, entertaining these nuances can be actively dangerous if realized, as a pause for reflection or hesitation can lead to the demise of one's self or comrades.

Instead, when conflict is imminent, or has already commenced, the idea of the other-as-enemy is bolstered by intensifying the threat posed by the enemy. If the enemy wins, so it is often stated, they could destroy those things that are held most dear: family, friends, children, principles, or home. Therefore, total force must be used to bring the

---

37. See Sebastian Junger, "We're All Guilty of Dehumanizing the Enemy," *The Washington Post*, January 13, 2012, https://www.washington-post.com/opinions/were-all-guilty-of-dehumanizing-the-ene-my/2012/01/13/gIQAtRduwP_story.html.

38. See History.com Editors, "Christmas Truce of 1914," *History*, October 27, 2009, https://www.history.com/topics/world-war-i/christ-mas-truce-of-1914.

enemy to complete subjugation, or even annihilation.[39] This position is maintained despite the possibility of the extraordinary loss of life, or the lasting psychological trauma that can be sustained by all parties involved in the conflict.[40]

As noted above, when Buchanan referenced the Cold War in his culture war rhetoric, when French likened left-leaning folks to terrorists, when Ahmari spoke of defeating the enemy and enjoying the spoils, or when others have drawn upon war as a metaphor to describe engagement in American culture, it is to these contours of the other-as-enemy—lacking dignity, inhuman, requiring complete destruction without distinction—that they are, at least indirectly, highlighting.

Compare this view of the 'other' as inherent in the war metaphor with some of the basic, far more nuanced, views Christians are called to maintain when they act as missionary disciples—views that flow directly from the Christian tradition and the witness of Christ himself.

A missionary view of the 'other' is that they contain an inherent value that cannot be ignored, suppressed, or rejected. Regardless of what they have done, where they live, what kind of threat they pose, or to which political party they belong, the other is, according to Christian anthropology, a child of God who has been made in the image of God (Gn. 1:27). Participation in the life of God is so essential to human beings, that it can never be completely lost. God always already holds the 'other' in existence.[41]

---

39. See Bernard Brodie and Rosalie West, ed., On War (Princeton: Princeton University Press, 1984), 75. Online at https://doi.org/10.2307/j.ctt7svzz.

40. See Richard Flanagan, The Narrow Road to the Deep North (New York: Penguin, 2013).

41. See Brett Salkeld, Transubstantiation: Theology, History, and Christian Unity (Grand Rapids: Baker, 2019), especially 35–55.

The other, moreover, is of such great value that, even despite the other's sinfulness and waywardness (that is, their inability to understand the world correctly, or to act according to God's plan), the Son of God, Jesus Christ, was willing to endure the humiliation of his passion, the torment of death on the cross, the nightmare of 'godforsakenness,' and the darkness of hell, because of the inherent value he saw in the other (cf. Heb. 12).[42] At a fundamental level, the 'other,' for God and, relatedly, for Christians, is an object worthy of love.

Jesus provides various parables that capture many of the nuances regarding the 'other' that Christians should maintain while engaging in mission that contradict the vision flowing from the war metaphor. Rather than being viewed as a threat requiring destruction, the other, according to the biblical tradition, is a lost sheep (Lk. 15:1-7), a prodigal son (Lk. 15:11-32), or a person beset by robbers (Lk. 10:29-37), in whom the Christian is invited to see *his own self* and, recognize that, *sans* the grace of God active in his own life, he himself could be in the same or a similar position (1 Cor. 15:10). In other words, only because of God's gift of grace is the Christian distinguishable from the very enemy that the war metaphor invites Christians to view as the one who needs to be destroyed *en mass*. In Jesus' far more nuanced view—one that rejects an easy black and white demarcation—the other as robber, prodigal son, or lost sheep deserves the Good News (Rm. 10:14), and is never completely removed from the opportunity to receive God's grace and love. Ultimately, the other has a soteriological value for Christians, as their own salvation is dependent

---

42. For a helpful analysis of some of these themes, see Hans Urs von Balthasar, *Mysterium Paschale: The Mystery of Easter*, trans. Aidan Nichols (San Francisco: Ignatius Press, 1990).

upon the way in which they treat the other with charity (Mt. 25:40).

Those are some foundational insights flowing from Christian missiology, which suggest the deficiency of the war metaphor in regards to the 'other.' These insights will be developed in subsequent chapters. Shifting the analysis, however, what about the ways that the war metaphor influences Christians to think specifically about missionary 'engagement' with the other?

The War Metaphor and Christian Missionary Engagement

In terms of how it can inform the nature of Christian engagement in mission, the war metaphor equally misses the mark.

Through the lens of war, Christian mission is predicated as the creation of bastions,[43] the placing of armaments, the construction of security measures, or the systematic use of killing mechanisms, all to reinforce separation from, bolster protection against, and, ultimately, destroy the enemy.[44] Throughout history, the tactics of war have changed, and these changes color the type of engagement encouraged by the war metaphor. Engagement can include annihilating one's enemy—and even oneself—as was frighteningly apparent during the Cold War; utilizing nefarious torture practices for coercion of one's enemy, as became part of the War on Terror;[45]

---

43. See Balthasar, *Razing the Bastions*.
44. See Brodie and West, *On War*, especially 223–276; 355–638.
45. See Jack Ruina, "Mutual Assured Destruction," *The New York Times*, June 30, 1974, https://www.nytimes.com/1974/06/30/archives/salt-in-a-mad-world-strategic-arms-limitation-talks-find-the.

or anonymous, distant, and, oftentimes, indiscriminately destructive killing of the other, as has become associated with modern drone warfare.[46]

Finally, and equally disturbing, once war has been initiated, diplomacy, dialogue, and compromise are often afterthoughts, difficult to introduce, and overshadowed by the destructive means of engagement of, and the vengeful feelings that linger from, war.[47]

Lakoff and Johnson's insight that metaphors have the ability to influence thought and action, and to do so in ways that are often unconscious, should not be forgotten here. It may seem that the types of engagement listed above are extreme. And, indeed, they are. Few people want to be reminded of the reality of Mutual Assured Destruction. But those who choose to use war as a metaphor in reference to Christian engagement invite, once again, at least indirectly, those who hear their words to imagine engaging with these dreadful tactics of war against the other in a religious-political conflict. Words have power, and metaphors can unconsciously influence thought and action.

---

html?searchResultPosition=3. See, also, Fred Kaplan, *The Bomb: Presidents, Generals, and the Secret History of Nuclear War* (New York: Simon and Shuster, 2020). See, also, Carol Rosenberg, "'20th Hijacker' is Returned to Saudi Arabia for Mental Health Care," *The New York Times*, March 7, 2022, https://www.nytimes.com/2022/03/07/us/politics/saudi-arabia-911-hijacker.html?searchResultPosition=7.

46. On some of the challenges related to drone warfare, see CNA Staff, "Vatican: Swarms of 'Kamikaze' Mini-Drones Pose Threat to Civilians," *Catholic News Agency*, August 6, 2021, https://www.catholicnewsagency.com/news/248605/vatican-swarms-of-kamikaze-mini-drones-pose-threat-to-civilians.

47. The recent war in Ukraine beginning in 2022 evidenced this reality. See Steven Erlanger and Patrick Kingsley, "As Diplomacy Drags on, Peace Seems Far Off in Ukraine," *The New York Times*, March 18, 2022, https://www.nytimes.com/2022/03/18/world/europe/ukraine-russia-peace-talks-diplomacy.html?searchResultPosition=6.

Again, contrast these forms of engagement that are part of war with some of the basic contours of Christian missionary engagement according to the tradition (contours that will receive specific treatment in subsequent chapters). Christian missionary engagement includes, rather than creating bastions in order to maintain distance, various forms of intimate, vulnerable, and close engagement with the other.[48] These are necessary so that a Christian can understand and know the other, so as to be able to minister to them, and to share with them the Good News. Rather than diplomacy being an afterthought, mission requires dialogue, conversation, and mutual sharing. This does not mean that these efforts of engagement will be straightforward, easy, or even fruitful. They might include Christians being misunderstood or outright rejected. Yet, even in the face of rejection, persecution, and possible martyrdom, Christian engagement involves the prudential encounter of the other so as to change hearts and invite the possibility of mutual conversion.[49] The witness of St. Francis of Assisi, as was visited in chapter three, provides evidence of the risk required by those who follow Christ who desire to share the gospel with all people—even with one's so-called enemy.

What is more, rather than defeat, destroy, or subjugate, Christians recognize that they can, and really must, learn from the so-called other as they engage in mission. The witness of the Church's saints, from Justin Martyr to Teresa of Kolkata (1910-1997), highlights this need.[50] Christians recognize that God, through his Spirit, always

---

48. Wessman, *Missionary Options for a Secular Age*, 193–194; 254–257; 334–335.

49. Wessman, *Missionary Options for a Secular Age*, 63–64.

50. See Bevans and Schroeder, *Constants in Context*, 84-86. See Mother Teresa, *No Greater Love* (Novato: New World Library, 1997).

already prepares the world for the reception of the gospel, planting 'seeds of the word' to facilitate this process. In order to share Jesus' love with the 'other,' Christians are required to discern the ways in which God has already been working in people's lives, perhaps in ways that are not always clearly evident without concerted, intentional, and intimate engagement. A vulnerable curiosity is necessary for Christians to discover the diverse ways that Jesus' grace is active in people's lives, even when it is not obviously apparent.[51]

Jesus' parables, as referred to above, provide ample evidence that, rather than hasty destruction of, or reckless, indiscriminate violence against, the other, Christian missionary engagement is something altogether different. Christians are called to provide succor and mercy to those beset by robbers. This is true even if the one lying in the ditch has been 'robbed' intellectually by succumbing to supposedly problematic ideologies or political perspectives (Lk. 10:34). It is difficult to attend to the wounds festering in others if one is motivated to inflict new wounds through metaphorical militaristic tactics of war. Christians, furthermore, are called to seek to bring back those who have gone astray, no matter how far the sheep have wandered into the hell of this world, or no matter how their actions have distanced them from God (cf. Lk. 15). Carrying a lost sheep back home is quite a different action than dropping metaphorical mortars to kill the 'sheep' on its wayward path. And, when the 'other' shows even minimal remorse for their actions, and hesitatingly, and perhaps through mixed motives, begins to return to God, Christians are to

---

51. On curiosity in engaging the other, see Mónica Guzmán, *I Never Thought of It That Way: How to Have Fearlessly Curious Conversations in Dangerously Divided Times* (Dallas: BenBella, 2022). See the discussion in chapter six below.

celebrate liberally with an abundant banquet, communing in joy with the very one whom, in a war metaphor, is often not even supposed to be viewed as human (cf. Lk. 15).

If the starkly contrasting vision of engagement presented in these parables does not convince Christians to eschew the war metaphor, Jesus' words regarding how Christians are to treat their enemies should invite them to put their metaphorical knife back in its sheath (cf. Jn. 18:10-12). Even if the other is deemed to be one's cultural enemy, and even if that person—that 'other'—is unwilling or unable to engage in a mutual exchange of ideas, gifts, or charity, rather than shoot, kill, bomb, blast, stab, or annihilate, Jesus' command is clear: Christians are to bless, pray for, and love their enemies (Mt. 5:44; Lk. 6:27-28).

Recapitulation

I have attempted to show above the ways in which the war metaphor 'highlights' and 'hides' various contours of Christian mission. Though the war metaphor does highlight somewhat accurately certain characteristics of mission, the Christian tradition provides its own grounding for these realities. This was the case in reference to the urgency that should be felt by Christians to engage in mission, and the sacrificial nature of discipleship. More importantly, however, the ways in which the metaphor of war can impede Christians from living the demands of the gospel are legion. These impediments are most obvious in the war metaphor's vision of the other, and the nature of engagement with the other this metaphor implies. Therefore, the war metaphor, as a tool to guide missionary activity is, at best, not necessary, and, at worst, detrimental to Christian discipleship.

Having spoken to many groups about what appears to be the blatant abuses inherent in using the war metaphor to guide Christian mission, I have come to realize that some people will continue to insist that war is an appropriate lens for Christians to use on account of the challenges facing the Church in the United States in the contemporary polarized milieu. The usual positions from those I have listened to are that the situation in the United States is so dire that only 'war' can elicit the proper response being required of Christians. Others state that the Christian tradition demands that Christians speak and defend the truth in the face of lies—a posture that the 'war metaphor' appropriately inspires.

Acknowledging these concerns, I want to be clear: I, too, recognize the challenges facing the Church in the United States. This book is a confession—that is, a labor of admission—that I, too, agree that both the United States and the Church in the United States are going through trying times. I also realize the importance of speaking the truth in love, especially to members of one's own communion who appear to have gone astray. I have encountered this as a pastor and leader of a religious order. Nevertheless, the times in which one lives as a Christian cannot be grounds for justifying every type of response in the face of the challenges of polarization, especially those that are not in line with the Christian tradition. (I will elaborate the complex options available to Christians in their response to the 'other' throughout the remainder of this book.)

My primary contention is that Christians cannot lose their identity in Christ, even as the hurricanes of polarization wreak havoc within the country and the Church, by informing their actions through the lens of war and enmity. There is too great a risk that those who use this metaphor will appropriate measures contrary to the tradition given by Jesus and the Church. Given that metaphors can have a seemingly unconscious or indirect influence on people, the risk only increases. Jesus was not naïve that his followers would face difficult times. He cautioned his disciples to be aware of wolves (Mt. 7:15), and he knew his message would not be received by all without the pains of conflict (Mt. 10:34). Nevertheless, in the face of strife, he warned that his followers would do the world no good if they did not adequately witness to the gospel. As he stated: If salt loses its taste, it is no longer good for anything (cf. Mt. 5:13).

What, then, is the metaphor that members of the Body of Christ should live by? When Christians return to their own sources, what is the vision provided to guide missionary discipleship? Though it is not possible to examine the entire tradition in the context of this book, the biblical witness of Paul's letter to the Philippians provides insight into how Christians can understand, and shape, their missionary action in the world. It is to the wisdom of St. Paul, and the metaphor he provides for Christian mission, that I now turn in the final section of this chapter. After briefly introducing Paul's proposed metaphor, the deeper implications of this metaphor will be explored in the remaining chapters of this book.

The Metaphor for Christians to Live By: Jesus' Incarnational Movement

Following his conversion to Jesus Christ, Paul labored to establish many Christian communities, one being in Philippi. A trading city in Macedonia, slightly inland from the Aegean Sea, and located on the Via Egnatia, Philippi was likely visited by Paul around the year 50 while on his

Second Missionary Journey.[52] The small Christian group Paul planted in the city would become his first church in Europe, and would be a thriving community nearly a century later.[53] After establishing the *ekklesia*, Paul moved on to other missionary endeavors. Nonetheless, he would maintain contact with the people at Philippi, and the Letter to the Philippians is evidence of this communication.

The context for this letter is important to consider in light of this present book's theme.[54] Paul is writing from prison and has flirted with his own death on account of the threatening world in which he lives. He is being punished for his beliefs and is suffering because he was willing to preach the gospel even despite the risk. The community he is writing to is facing many hardships as well, including various forms of persecution. Most likely these are coming from civic authorities, members of the non-Christian public, and Jewish Christians opposing Paul's message.[55] In addition to this externally inflicted tumult, there is disunity within the Philippian community itself, as the bonds of *koinōnia* are being stretched to the point of tearing.

Sound familiar? The cultural context in Philippi was not unlike the situation experienced by the Church in the United States today: external pressures placed on Christians to conform to the mentality of the outside world; persecution of those who are bravely attempting to the live the gospel in the public arena; and strife, division, and, well, yes, polarization, within the Christian commu-

---

52. See Raymond E. Brown, *An Introduction to the New Testament* (New York: Doubleday, 1997), 483–484.

53. Ibid.

54. John Barton and John Muddiman, ed., *The Oxford Biblical Commentary* (Oxford: Oxford University Press, 2001), 1179–1190.

55. See Barton and Muddiman, *The Oxford*, 1179. See, also, Brown, *An Introduction*, 483–489.

nity itself. Although 2000 years have passed, these challenges remain, of course with their own variations.

It seems that, given everything he was enduring personally, and given what he knew was happening to the community at Philippi, Paul would have had every reason in this volatile, challenging, and divisive moment to utilize 'war' as a metaphor to guide the Christian community to self-preservation and stability. Paul was not averse to referring to the virtues that went along with military commitment (2 Tm. 2:3-4). He wrote, moreover, about 'spiritual warfare,' and the need to defeat principalities and powers, even if these comments primarily addressed the spiritual realm (cf. 2 Cor. 10:1-6; Rm. 8:37-39). He even mentions in his letter to the community at Philippi that he is sending a "fellow soldier" back to the community in Epaphroditus, who was possibly a military man (Phil. 2:25). Nevertheless, when providing a metaphor for Christian missionary discipleship, to be lived both within, and outside of, the Christian community, Paul does not turn to the intoxicatingly tempting metaphor of war. Instead, he turns to a common hymn in the early Church to provide the metaphor for Christians to live by.

What metaphor does Paul suggest? He proposes Jesus' incarnational movement—his *kenosis*—his self-emptying movement into the created world through his incarnation and extended beyond into his ministry, passion, death, and resurrection. Christians are to be motivated in their discipleship to have the "same mind" as their savior, adopting his mentality toward the world.[56] As Paul states, quoting extensively an early Christian hymn:

---

56. This short reference provides another way of interpreting Paul's words. See Barton and Muddiman, *The Oxford*, 1184.

Have among yourselves the same attitude that is also yours in Christ Jesus,

Who, though he was in the form of God, did not regard equality with God something to be grasped. Rather, he emptied himself, taking the form of a slave, coming in human likeness, and found human in appearance, he humbled himself, becoming obedient to death, even death on a cross (Phil. 2:5-8).

In the face of the endemic suffering, sinfulness, danger, and the sadness of the world, the Son of God did not forsake the created world, placing 'distance' between himself and this world. Neither did he choose to obliterate the world. He did not even choose to condemn the world, even though, in justice, this response was warranted. Instead, he chose to draw close to the world, to embrace the world in all things but sin, and to take the risk required to stand in solidarity with a broken world. And why did he do this? Because he loved the world, and desired to save it (Jn. 3:16-21).

It was this mentality toward the world that Paul was inviting Christians to consider as the form and example of discipleship. If Jesus humbled himself and crossed over into a complicated and dangerous world, Christians were being called to do the same. If Jesus emptied himself by embracing the outcasts and marginalized people of this world, Christians were called to embrace and encounter the other in an analogous way. If Jesus risked his own life out of love for all people, Christians were challenged to consider, in prudence, how they could do the same.

Paul was convinced that, if the believers at Philippi were to have the same mind as Christ—i.e., if they appropriated the metaphor of Christ's *kenosis* as seen through his incarnational movement—these efforts would have the effect of instantiating more fully the very kingdom of God

that Jesus initiated, and that Christians vigorously anticipated. As Paul states, through kenotic discipleship:

> [At] the name of Jesus every knee should bend, of those
> in heaven and on earth and under the earth, and every
> tongue confess that Jesus Christ is Lord, to the glory of
> God the Father (Phil. 2:10-11).

Christian appropriation of Christ's incarnational movement would fulfill Jesus' own redemptive work by bringing
the possibility of salvation to all people.

Many implications flow from this early Christian
hymn. The hands of the Church's greatest theologians have
written extensively about it.[57] What is clear, however, and
what will be the content of the remainder of this book, is
that the wisdom contained in this hymn, and in the words
of St. Paul, presents a different vision for missionary discipleship than that provided by the war metaphor. Christ's
kenotic movement, his willingness to risk *crossing over*
into the created realm out of love for all creation, to stand
in solidarity with, so as to *encounter*, the world, and to do
so to the point of death, thereby *inviting* the world to enjoy
the possibility of participating in his divine life and *salvation*, was proposed as the Christian form and example for
mission and evangelization.[58] As Christ entered the chaos
of the world, he called Christians to enter the storms of life
with him, to deepen his salvation in a tempestuous world.

These two themes, *crossing over*, and *salvific encounter*, will occupy the remaining chapters of this book as I
explore what Christ's incarnational movement entails for
Christian mission in a polarized world.

---

57. See Mark J. Edwards, ed., *Ancient Christian Commentary on Scripture: New Testament VIII: Galatians, Ephesians, Philippians* (Downers
Grove: InterVarsity Press, 1999), especially 236-260.
58. See Barton and Muddiman, *The Oxford*, 1184.

ꟿ

Chapter Five

Discipleship as Crossing Over

Crossing into the Storm to Save Lives

It's three in the morning on Tuesday, September 11th, 2018.[1] While most of the southeast United States is fast asleep, members of the Air Force's Hurricane Hunter Team are wide awake. It is their 'busy season,' and Hurricane Florence is ominously approaching the coasts of the Carolinas.

The crew meets on a runway in Savannah, Georgia, and boards a plane. The engines of the 'Hurricane Hunter' begin to hum as the crew prepares for takeoff. For those unaccustomed to habitual acts of bravery, flying west, away from the mammoth weather system building over the

---

1. For more on this story, see the following video: WSJ Video, "Take a Flight With the Hurricane Hunters Chasing a Storm," *The Wall Street Journal*, September 13, 2018, https://www.wsj.com/video/take-a-flight-with-the-hurricane-hunters-chasing-a-storm/19C13265-0503-4F75-B309-94FADE82E549.html. See, also, Valerie Bauerlein, "In a Plane, Flying Through the Eye of Hurricane Florence," September 13, 2018, https://www.wsj.com/articles/in-a-plane-flying-through-the-eye-of-hurricane-florence-1536836400.

Atlantic, would be preferred. However, this plane, along with its crew, are going east, directly toward the storm.

The crew appears astonishingly calm. They check instruments, adjust equipment, and acknowledge the media personnel documenting the flight. Given the immensity of the beast they are approaching, with its intense winds, blinding lightning, and lake-sized volumes of moisture,[2] their serenity bespeaks an internal fortitude. They are resolutely determined to do their job.

The immediate end of the mission is to collect data. Both through the many sensors decorating the aircraft, and the 'dropsonde' capsules that are released through launch tubes out into the storm, the crew seeks to learn as much about the nature of the system as possible, so as to predict its patterns and trajectory. They carefully maneuver the plane, passing in and out of the 'eye,' repeating this process, until they have collected enough data.

Most human beings would likely be satisfied not participating in this mission or braving no more than one trip on this plane. If they survived, at least it would make for an unmatchable story at cocktail hour. However, this crew of hurricane hunters has made storm chasing their life. Whenever systems approach, they fly constantly, 24-7, only stopping to refuel and, if they are lucky, to rest.

Why, ultimately, might one ask, are they crossing over into hurricanes when, let's be honest, it seems just a little crazy? The answer is simple: to save lives. The data they collect is not only scientifically interesting, but it can also literally save the lives of those potentially caught in the path of the storm. So, they continue to engage storm after

---

2. See Robinson Meyer, "Florence Will Drop an Inconceivable Amount of Water," *The Atlantic*, September 14, 2018, https://www.theatlantic.com/science/archive/2018/09/hurricane-florence-the-deluge-begins/570370/.

storm, learning from their experiences, and risking their own lives so that others may live.

At the outset of this chapter, I want to be upfront about the argument I am going to make. Stemming from the previous chapter's glimpse into Christ's *kenotic* movement, I will reason that Christians who have found new life in Christ are being called to cultivate similar dispositions of courage and bravery as those maintained by the Hurricane Hunters, and to cross over into the storms of polarized groups. Not only is 'crossing over,' as will be shown, necessary in an age of polarization. But I will argue that it is fundamental to missionary discipleship.

To unpack the contents of this argument, this chapter will proceed as follows.

I will begin by highlighting the cost of discipleship, especially in a polarized age. I do not want to appear naïve regarding the sacrifice that is required to live a life of 'crossing over.' It will likely be tough, disorienting, dangerous and, at times, emotionally intense. In many ways, like hurricane hunters flying into storms, one who follows Jesus in a life of 'crossing over' will be risking nearly everything.

Even despite the costs, however, a life of crossing over is necessary. I will explore this necessity by highlighting research that indicates how actions of crossing over are vital to overcoming some of the negative effects of polarization. More importantly, however, at least for Christians, I will demonstrate how crossing over is essential for a life of discipleship. The fundamental importance of crossing over for Christians becomes clear in an analysis of Jesus' own life, which provides the example for all Christian discipleship.

To begin my argument, it is important to look at what is meant by the 'cost of discipleship.' A fitting way to do so is to turn to a time and a place where so many people, including Christians, paid the highest price by giving their lives in the face of grotesque evil: Germany in the 1930s and 40s.

The Cost of Missionary Discipleship

Born in 1906 in Breslau, Germany, Dietrich Bonhoeffer would mature as a Christian under the dark shadows of Nazism. Committed wholeheartedly to following Jesus, Bonhoeffer would realize that discipleship, for him, would mean confronting the great evils of Adolf Hitler's Third Reich. Focusing on the theme of discipleship in his own writings, this minister and theologian would extensively reflect upon the 'costliness' of discipleship. He would later be required to witness to the truth of his own theology. In April of 1945, at the young age of 39, on account of his willingness to 'cross over' and persistently and publicly engage with, and critique, the Nazi Regime, and those who were hypnotized by its allure, Bonhoeffer would be executed at the Flossenbürg concentration camp in Bavaria.

Bonhoeffer's legacy, both his writings and lived example—that is, in his willingness to challenge the horrors of Nazism, and to risk his own life in doing so—harmoniously flowed from his theological understanding of Christian life. Discipleship, according to him, was costly because, on the one hand, the grace required to follow Jesus came at a great price. In his famous work *The Cost of Discipleship*, he wrote: "Above all, grace is costly, because it was costly to God, because it costs God the life of God's Son—'you were bought with a price'—and because nothing can be cheap to us which is costly to God."[3] Discipleship is costly, on the other

---

3.   Dietrich Bonhoeffer, et al., *Discipleship* (Minneapolis: Fortress Press, 2001), 45.

hand, because it requires those who follow Jesus to imitate their savior by giving of themselves totally and freely—in some cases even giving their biological lives over in death. Bonhoeffer was unambiguous on this point. "Whenever Christ calls us," he wrote, "his call leads us to death."[4]

Bonhoeffer's insight here is helpful in framing the theme of this chapter. Following Christ by crossing over into the hurricanes of polarization will be costly for those who choose to do so. To be clear, I am not comparing the contemporary situation in the United States to early-to-mid-twentieth century Germany, and neither am I suggesting that all people will face martyrdom by living a life of missionary discipleship modeled on 'crossing over.' Nevertheless, there will be great sacrifices required of those who follow Jesus in the contemporary period, move into the tempests of polarized hurricanes, and bravely encounter the other. To think differently is to ignore the words and example of Jesus, and the great Cloud of Witnesses, including Bonhoeffer, who have understood the cost of discipleship throughout the ages. It is also to ignore much research on the challenges related to polarization.

The Costs of Crossing Over

What, specifically, are the potential challenges, sacrifices, and even suffering, that can be involved in the experience of crossing over into the storm of one's out-group? At a minimum, people will have to accept the reality that crossing over is going to mean choosing to be uncomfortable, and regularly opting to feel out of place.[5]

---

4. Bonhoeffer, *Discipleship*, 87.
5. On this point, see Holland and Silvers, *I Think You're Wrong*, 132–157.

Americans have, as was documented in chapter one, sorted themselves into groups of like-minded people. This is understandable. People often prefer to sort themselves into groups, so as to be around others who think and act like them. There is actually a word for this: homophily, i.e., the love of sameness.[6] It is oftentimes just easier and, well, more enjoyable to be around people who share one's interests, viewpoints, and hobbies. It can be life giving.

As Mónica Guzmán, in her wonderfully written book on polarization, states: "If there's one law of human nature that rules them all these days, it's that it's way, *way* easier to like people who are like us."[7] She continues: "We go near people who share our interests for reasons we feel and know and appreciate. Sorting makes us happier, less bothered, more content, and more linked."[8] She's right, and choosing to cross over will mean choosing to work against this internal desire for comfort, the attraction of sorting, and the pull of homophily that have become commonplace today.

This is no easy task, to be sure. I think it is safe to say that most people gravitate toward comfort rather than discomfort. Breaking this pattern will require effort.[9] But it gets more difficult. 'Crossing over' will also involve choosing a somewhat more psychologically and spiritually fragile, vulnerable existence, and to do so in an age already filled with fragility.

As was explored in chapter two, people's groups, tribes, or families often provide them with psychological

---

6. Guzmán, *I Never Thought*, 5.
7. Guzmán, *I Never Thought*, 3.
8. Guzmán, *I Never Thought*, 5.
9. Holland and Silvers, *I Think You're Wrong*, 132–133.

stability, identity, and feelings of safety.[10] Human beings have been made to belong to groups, and they feel most 'at home' within groups. In an age of intense fragility, as was explored above, these groups become even more important to people. They are places of relative calm amid the storm of life, and they are sources of support amid a world lacking the same. And part of what bolsters feelings of safety, and one's sense of identity within groups is, sadly, viewing those outside of the group as the 'other.'[11] In one sense, people can even create greater cohesion by labeling others as, well, 'other.'[12]

To select to cross over will mean to choose to leave the safety of one's own group, to shun, at least temporarily, many of the psychological comforts that come with one's group identities, to step into a world of liminality where one's identity is not reinforced by those they are around, and to set aside some of the 'othering' tendencies that often strengthen in-group dynamics.[13] People will have to choose to see, and embrace, something valuable in relating to out-group members, even as they feel their fragility in this world increase through this very practice.[14]

I suspect that for many Christians reading this book, the concern raised above strikes a chord. There is a danger that, in crossing over, Christians may experience the ero-

---

10. Guzmán, I Never Thought, 2. See, also, chapter two.
11. Guzmán, I Never Thought, 17–30.
12. See Jacobs, How to Think, 24–28.
13. See Holland and Silvers, I Think You're Wrong, 158–173. See, also, Justin Lee, Talking Across the Divide: How to Communicate with People You Disagree with and Maybe Even Change the World (New York: TarcherPerigee, 2018), 85–99.
14. See Jacobs, How to Think, 139–151. For insight into what 'crossing over' can mean in the legal profession, see, for instance, Robert K. Vischer, "Legal Education in an Age of Polarization," University of St. Thomas Law Journal, forthcoming.

sion of the foundation of life in Christ upon which they stand. One's ecclesial community can provide a haven in an ever-increasingly non-believing world. Stepping out of that community and crossing over into 'the world' presents real challenges to maintaining Christian identity. And yet, even though the concern of losing one's identity in Christ by crossing over is legitimate, it seems that choosing not to cross over may be just as detrimental to one's life of discipleship. More on this point will follow.

For most people, and not just for Christians, feelings of fragility and a desire for group belonging are wired deep within them, are intensified by the effects of the Fall—as seen through a theological perspective (see chapter two), and exert a significant influence on them, such that breaking out of one's group to cross over will be no easy task. And the challenges only become more acute.

People's choice to cross over does not solely affect them as individuals. It also can affect each of the members within their own in-group.[15]

By choosing, at least temporarily, to leave their group and to engage with another, a person will likely learn from the experience. She will ask different questions, view the 'other' in new, perhaps favorable, ways, refashion her identity, and readjust her vision of the world.[16] When she 'returns' to her own in-group, she will necessarily, by her very presence, bring this newness into her own group. Others, whether they like it or not, will be forced to deal within their group with the presence of new ways of thinking, different experiences of the world, and slightly modified perspectives of reality.[17]

---

15. See Jacobs, *How to Think*, 20–24.
16. See Guzmán, *I Never Thought*, 43.
17. A novel that captures the tension related to this theme is Pat Con-

Not everyone is going to enjoy the new viewpoints offered, nor the instability introduced in the group. They might even dislike them—and despise the person who crossed over for exposing them to further fragility in a fragile world. If there is an adage that remains true for many people, it is that change is not easy to accept. It is one thing to open oneself to the temporary disorientation and anxiety that accompany the engagement of new ideas, people, and experiences; it is another to introduce these to others.

What this means, then, is not only will a person who crosses over be unsure of how she will be received by those she crosses over to engage, she will also likely face rejection from her own in-group. She could even lose friends and loved ones.[18]

This latter type of rejection—by one's own in-group—has become a significant phenomenon within various places of cultural exchange today, such as through social or traditional media, on college campuses, or in academic circles.[19] When members of one group see that members of their own group are not actively dismissing or intensely demonizing the other mega-group, let alone actually seeking to encounter, understand, or even learn from members of the out-group, they can become the object of derision in their own group.[20] Inter alia, one recalls here the example from chapter four of the ire David French faced within his own conservative circle for espousing even a slight 'openness' to remain civil toward his fellow citizens coming from a different mega-group.[21]

---

roy's The Prince of Tides (Boston: Houghton Mifflin Company, 1986).

18. Jacobs, How to Think, 150.
19. See Jacobs, How to Think, 23–28.
20. See Haidt, "Why the Past."
21. See Ahmari, "Against David." See, also, Lukianoff and Haidt, The Coddling of the American.

Social psychologist Jonathan Haidt has written on the subject regarding the kind of rejection people can face from their own in-group by branching out. He states that those who flirt with crossing over find it "hazardous to be seen fraternizing with the enemy or even failing to attack the enemy with sufficient vigor."[22] They become targeted by those within their own group, and fear that they will be 'called out' for not taking a more intensified, negative approach to the other.[23]

These concerns are real. And those who choose to engage the 'other' will most likely have to contend with them. However, for most people, the challenges listed above probably pale in comparison to what can be encountered when one *actually* crosses over into the other megagroup hurricane and meets the out-group other.

Once the other is encountered, the uncertainty of this moment is enough to discourage most people from ever crossing over. It is not by chance that people today do not even want to get together over the holidays with family members who identify with the out-group.[24] It has become too risky, too difficult, and too painful. The uncertainty felt today of even sitting down at the table with someone from another political or ecclesial tribe is immense.

Like Hurricane Hunters passing through a storm, crossing over into a polarized group will likely introduce much turbulence. Not only is there the real possibility of having to contend with the reality that one's vision of the

---

22. See Haidt, "Why the Past."
23. See Lukianoff and Haidt, The Coddling of the American, 81–121.
24. See Richard Schiffman, "How to Handle Difficult Conversations at Thanksgiving: Should Families Take Politics Off the Table this Year," The New York Times, November 20, 2018, https://www.nytimes.com/2018/11/20/well/family/thanksgiving-partisan-politics-conversations-families.html.

world was incorrect and needs to be adjusted—i.e., *that one was wrong*—encountering the out-group is unpredictable. It can include rejection, humiliation, misunderstanding and, in extreme cases, emotional or physical harm, and even death. These latter experiences are certainly uncommon, but still a possibility. The Internet today is filled with stories and videos depicting the encounter between different tribes, and the scenes are not pretty.[25] This is not to say that helpful, illuminating, and life-changing encounters between people of different tribes are not possible.[26] Indeed, many people are committed to these exchanges today, and the dialogue and sharing are bearing much fruit (more on this later).[27]

Nevertheless, no one really knows what outcome will result from entering into the opposition's polarized hurricane, and many people will ultimately decide not to embrace 'crossing over' actions in their life because of the potential risks. Why risk so much to stand in solidarity with someone who threatens one's entire way of being, who holds nearly unbridgeable views of the most important

---

25. A particularly sad encounter took place in Charlottesville, VA. See Laurel Wamsley and Bobby Allyn, "Neo-Nazi Who Killed Charlottesville Protester is Sentenced to Life in Prison," NPR, June 28, 2019, https://www.npr.org/2019/06/28/736915323/neo-nazi-who-killed-charlottesville-protester-is-sentenced-to-life-in-prison. See, also, Jacobs, *How to Think*. See, also, Adam Grant, *Think Again: The Power of Knowing What You Don't Know* (New York: Viking, 2021). See, also, Lukianoff and Haidt, *The Coddling of the American*.

26. For a few examples, visit https://braverangels.org/ or https://catholicsocialthought.georgetown.edu/. See, also, https://icccr.tc.columbia.edu/research/.

27. See Guzmán, *I Never Thought*. For an insightful example of how two people from different political groups can have a meaningful conversation, see The Ezra Klein Show, "Transcript: Ezra Klein Interviews Patrick Deneen," *The New York Times*, May 13, 2022, https://www.nytimes.com/2022/05/13/podcasts/transcript-ezra-klein-interviews-patrick-deneen.html.

contours of life, who has even said mean-spirited or hate-ful comments targeting the values and identities which are the most meaningful to people in their life, or who perhaps poses a threat to one's own life?

I admit that the above question is difficult to answer. I think that each person must discern this question in his or her own life. And I hope that I have not lost readers by spending hundreds of words emphasizing the real challenges that exist by taking up this aspect of discipleship. It is important to be forthright about the costs. However, even though the challenges exist, a lot of research is being published highlighting *why* crossing over is worth the risk.

Hoping that people will consider the gamble, it is to this research that I now turn.

The Importance of Crossing Over: Some Preliminary Considerations

Adam Grant's *Think Again* is an ode to thinking, or, perhaps more accurately, 'rethinking.' In this masterful work, he explores how human beings reason, the impediments that exist to thinking clearly, and how people can be challenged to, as his title suggests, 'think again,' that is, to move beyond their biases or ideological limitations in order to understand more deeply the truthfulness of the world around them. One of the most remarkable capacities of human beings is the ability to think. It is just that, unfortunately, as Grant's research demonstrates, human beings do not always think well.

An insightful contour of Grant's research, particularly for this present discussion, is his exploration concerning the issue of personal bias.[28] Grant seeks to understand how human beings might overcome, or at least acknowledge and reexamine, the biases that impede them from viewing the world more truthfully. Poring over research, Grant's goal is to understand how "to break overconfidence cycles [i.e., ways of thinking that can miss the mark on reality] that are steeped in stereotypes and prejudices about entire groups of people."[29] In other words, he wants to shine light on how to overcome some of the challenges of polarization—the intensifying hatred toward, mistrust of, and misunderstanding about out-group members.

Though it is beyond the purpose of this section to go through all the research Grant presents (I highly recommend reading his book), his conclusion regarding the aforementioned theme is germane. When assessing the many ways people can attempt to overcome biases and better relate to out-group members, from seeking to build greater understanding by finding common interests with members of another group, endeavoring to empathize with another group by understanding their situation in life, recognizing the contingency of one's own beliefs, or becoming accustomed to the thought processes of out-group members, it is crossing over and engaging the other *in person* that is most likely to produce the desired result.[30] I want to state this again: only in crossing over is there significant evidence that one could begin to see the world, especially the 'other,' more truthfully, or at least in a more favorable light. Here is Grant at length:

---

28. See Grant, *Think Again*, 121–141.
29. Grant, *Think Again*, 122.
30. Grant, *Think Again*, 128–136.

Sometimes letting go of stereotypes means realizing that many members of a hated group aren't so terrible after all. And that's more likely to happen when we actually come face-to-face with them. For over half a century, social scientists have tested the effects of intergroup contact [i.e., crossing over to meet the 'other']. In a meta-analysis of over five hundred studies with over 250,000 participants, interacting with members of another group reduced prejudice in 94 percent of the cases. Although intergroup communication isn't a panacea, that is a staggering statistic.[31]

I agree. It is difficult to overstate the imperative flowing from the meaning of these words by Grant. To overcome the negative tendencies that can emerge from polarization, crossing over is not only vital—it might be one of the only methods that can nearly guarantee the lessening of bias or prejudice, and the deepening of understanding, between in-group and out-group members.

Grant is not alone among researchers of polarization who have landed on this point. Mónica Guzmán, for example, in her extensive writing on the contributing factors, along with the possible solutions regarding, polarization, notes the research cited by Grant.[32] Guzmán, moreover, provides an incisive reflection as to what potentially can take place in crossing over that can reduce the negative effects of polarization.

According to Guzmán, crossing over can help to humanize the other.[33] When people cross over and

---

31. Grant, *Think Again*, 139.
32. Guzmán, *I Never Thought*, 45.
33. See Guzmán, *I Never Thought*, 45-47. See, also, Charlie Camosy, "Eden Invitation Wants to Help the Church Look 'Beyond the LGBT

encounter the other, especially when this is done person-to-person, either in small groups or in pairs,[34] people are often reminded that more than ideas are at stake within the polarized hurricanes of the American context. Within each hurricane exists real, actual people. The people in either hurricane may hold staggeringly different viewpoints; but no one can be reduced to those viewpoints. The individuals holding divergent views are authentic, living, breathing members of the same human family, who have hopes, dreams, and desires, many that are likely mutually shared between in-group and out-group members.[35] When one chooses to encounter the other, the likelihood of seeing the *person* who espouses the idea, and not just the idea that one disagrees with, becomes more likely.

As Guzmán states: "We don't interact with ideas, causes, or beliefs...The way I see it, we interact only with each other. We sort into our groups, push off our *others*, and settle in, too often and too deeply, to silos that keep us from seeing each other for who we really are."[36] One of the ways to see that a hurricane formed in a polarizing context is not solely a hurricane of supposed 'dangerous' ideas, is to cross over into it, and to find waiting there other human

---

Paradigm.' Here's How," *The Pillar*, May 13, 2022, https://www.pillar-catholic.com/p/how-eden-invitation-wants-to-help?s=r.

34. For more on the importance of engaging people from the 'out-group' in small groups or, especially, in pairs, see Amy Uelmen, "Who Does Jesus Call Our Christian Churches to be in a Polarized Society?" unpublished paper given at the Christian Churches Together Conference, October 4, 2022. See, also, Amy Uelmen, "To Walk in Our Divided Political Land, Try Buddy System," *Catholic Philly*, September 11, 2020, https://catholicphilly.com/2020/09/commentaries/to-walk-in-our-divided-political-land-try-buddy-system/.

35. I highly recommend, once again (see footnote above), this podcast episode of The Ezra Klein Show where he interviews conservative thinker Patrick Deneen.

36. Guzmán, *I Never Thought*, 46.

beings—people with dignity; people with hopes; people much like the one who has just chosen to cross over.

The Importance of Crossing Over: The Example of Jesus

Having begun to weigh the benefits and costs of engaging a perceived 'other,' I suspect that, for some people, the scale likely continues to tip toward the costs. I have no doubt that most readers of this book are genuinely concerned about the effects of polarization. But I can imagine that they continue to maintain that the risks involved in crossing over are still too many, and too ominous. Though I am personally passionate about the necessity of crossing over (even as I struggle to instantiate this in my own life), I can appreciate that some would come to this latter conclusion.

For Christians reading this book, however, I want to attempt to tip the scale, ever so gently, just a little more in favor of crossing boundaries, by providing an abundance of evidence from specifically Christian presuppositions.[37] In what follows, I am going to attempt to substantiate the argument that, for Christians, crossing over is not really an option: It is essential to a life of missionary discipleship.

Allow me to pause here and note that I realize that what I state above sounds a lot like a moral imperative for Christian living. I also recognize that fully justifying an imperative is difficult to do. And, I want to be clear: I am distinguishing between *how* one is called to cross over from the question of *whether or not* intergroup engage-

---

37. Other research is being conducted showing the resourcefulness of Christianity in the face of polarization. See, for instance, a forthcoming article by James Cavendish, "Religion as a Resource in an Increasingly Polarized Society," *Sociology of Religion*, forthcoming.

ment should be an integral part of a disciple's life. I am concerned here with the latter. But the evidence that crossing over is foundational to a life of discipleship is ample. Jesus' own life, after which Christians, à la Paul (see chapter four), are to model their own missionary activity, tips the scale.

To defend this somewhat bold assertion, I will explore three 'moments' in Jesus' life: 1) the Son of God crossing over in the incarnation; 2) Jesus crossing over during his public ministry; and 3) the 'crossing over' involved in the mysteries of Jesus' passion and death.

The Son of God Crossing Over in the Incarnation

To understand the depth of God's love for human beings and, also, the gratuitous, and unconditional loving action of the Son of God in his willingness to cross over to save the world, I invite readers to 'put on the mind of Christ' with me, and to imagine God's view of the world, and what it would have meant for God to choose to cross over into the created world through the incarnation. I admit that I will include some theological speculation here, as well as a certain anthropomorphizing of God. But I hope readers permit me this license so that I can show the extent to which crossing over is consistent with God's *entire approach to world*.[38]

Imagine God looking upon creation. Since he is eternal, 'standing' outside of time, he has a vision of the full breadth of time—all that has existed, all that exists, and all

---

38. For more on this theme, see Balthasar, *Razing the Bastions*. See, also, Hans Urs von Balthasar, "Kenosis of the Church?" in *Explorations in Theology IV: Spirit and Institution*, trans. Edward T. Oakes, S.J. (San Francisco: Ignatius, 1995), 125–138.

that will exist. What does he see? No doubt, he comprehends the beauty of creation, the joys and happiness of life, and the bouquet of love that is shared between people. But, to be sure, he also observes the people he created, those bearing his image (Gn. 1:27), struggling in a valley of tears.

Think of the great tragedies of history.[39] Wars. Genocides. Hatred. Holocausts. Polarization. The destruction of the Earth. Murder of innocents. The sadness, brokenness, weakness, and fragility of the human experience. These are not just theoretical tragedies, but ones that touch intimately and uniquely the lives of each human being, evoking real tears and eliciting intense suffering, none of which goes unnoticed by God. All this is viewed through the eyes of a God who truly loves what he has created with a love that is, well, difficult to imagine. In as much as it is possible to attribute human feelings to God, one can say that God's heart is moved by the tragic affairs within creation—because he truly loves those who are suffering, struggling, and unable to find their way (Mt. 9:36; Ps. 34).

And yet, God does not 'stand' idly by and observe humanity's floundering but, rather, acts to restore all things to an even greater glory.

In and through his love, God seeks to help humanity. While respecting free will, he raises up a Chosen People (Gn. 12), he acts to release those in slavery (e.g. Ex. 3:7), he leads prophets so that they in turn can guide human beings back to God (e.g. Is. 6), he provides a loving law by which to form human action (Ex. 20), and he offers, time and

---

39. On this point, see, for instance, Ian Kershaw, *To Hell and Back: Europe 1914–1949* (London: Penguin, 2015). See, also, N.T. Wright, *God and the Pandemic: A Christian Reflection on the Coronavirus and Its Aftermath* (Grand Rapids: Zondervan Reflective, 2020).

again, new covenants to his people.[40] That is, he unwaveringly reaches out to humanity to reestablish a relationship with them, wanting to be in solidarity with them as they struggle, and to transform what has been lost. God looks upon creation, comprehends the dire straits that exist, and attempts to save his people.

It is just that human beings cannot seem to follow through. They are given opportunity after opportunity to amend their ways, to choose the good, and to put aside the atrocities and horrors of existence; yet, they continue to reject the olive branch given by God. So wars rage, horrors continue, and existence is shattered.[41]

At this 'moment,' it is understandable that God would choose to give up on creation. Few could blame him. Countless attempts spanning millennia to rescue fallen humanity are quite the effort. "Why should I keep trying?" we imagine God saying. "It is not possible to save these lost souls."[42] In justice, God is right in condemning creation— God does not owe creation anything, and is honoring people's free choices to reject his help and love (Rm. 6:23).

And here is the point where the splendor of God shines forth in its great magnificence. Here is where saint after saint has looked upon God and fallen in love with a Creator who was willing to cross over to save everyone. Even after the constant rejections, the horrors of murder, the scandals of abuse, the endless wars, the storms of polarization, and the arrogance and pride of a people building towers to

---

40. For a beautiful depiction of the history of salvation, and God's endless offer of friendship to God's people, see Eucharistic Prayer IV of the *Roman Missal*.
41. For a helpful discussion regarding this tension, see St. Augustine, *The Confessions* (Peabody: Hendrickson Christian Classics, 2004).
42. For a wonderful depiction of God wrestling with creation and people's waywardness, see Gn. 18.

heaven while they sink in the mire of their stupor (Gn. 11:1-9; Ps. 40:2), God chooses to enter the great drama of life.[43] He takes on flesh and is born of Mary (Jn. 1:14). He sees the storm, he knows full well the cost, and he chooses to pass right into the midst of it to save his people.

The incarnation is a profound mystery of the Christian faith. What transpires in this mystery is only possible through the action of God. Christians do not really know *how* this mystery is carried out except that it is done through God's loving action, in cooperation with Mary's open reception of grace (Lk. 1:26-38).[44]

Nevertheless, it is possible to speculate about the *meaning* of God's willingness to cross over into creation through this mystery. The Son of God knows full well the tragedy of human life. It isn't pretty. And yet, rather than fleeing, he does the opposite. He decides to unite himself *more intimately* with the human experience. More intimately! He decides to take on flesh and unite himself with every reality that created existence entails, save for personal sinfulness: joy, peace, happiness, and love, *along with* sadness, liminality, decay, suffering, rejection, mortality, and even death (Heb. 4:15).

Swiss theologian Hans Urs von Balthasar (1905–1988), a Christian author who was thoroughly committed to plumbing the depths of meaning in Christ's incarnation and his *kenotic* love, captures the wonder of the mystery of the incarnation in stating:

---

43. See Hans Urs von Balthasar, *Engagement with God: The Drama of Christian Discipleship*, trans. R. John Halliburton (San Francisco: Ignatius Press, 1986).

44. On the difference between the 'how' of a mystery, and the 'what' of a mystery, see Salkeld, *Transubstantiation*, 75–76.

[Through the incarnation,] God steps into this so very worldly world, so dissimilar to God, and claims it for himself, precisely in this worldliness and dissimilarity. The very feature that makes the world the world, its naturalness with all that this means—reasoning, logical thinking, free will, sympathetic feeling, the vitality and animality of man's physicality, his emotions, pains and desires, in short the whole great bazaar of everyday life on earth—has been sought out by God as *the* place for his incarnation.[45]

Balthasar's words here are apt: God does not shy away from the horrors within creation, but *seeks out this storm of existence*, not because he must, but because he loves us, and he desires to cross over in order to save us *in the storm* (cf. Mk. 4:35-41).

Even if one struggles to believe that God can or did become man (I do not want to presume upon the faith of readers, for faith is ultimately a mysterious gift), it is difficult to deny the attractiveness of the incarnation. The Son of God saw the disastrous state of affairs of the world and chose not to run away but, rather, to enter the mess more truly and profoundly in order to save us.

One can choose many different metaphors to try to approach this mystery, and never fully capture the beauty of the incarnation. For instance, the Son of God's movement in the incarnation is like a man running into a burning house to save the very one who intentionally started the fire; Jesus is like the one who leaves a lifeboat for raging waters to save a drowning woman who decided to go for a swim even though she was reminded that she knew not how; the Lord is like a soldier who goes behind enemy

---

45. Hans Urs von Balthasar, "The Fathers, the Scholastics, and Ourselves," *Communio* 24 (1997): 388.

lines to save a prisoner of war who previously fled from the battle in the midst of intense fighting; Christ is like the one who trades his own life for the life of his enemy who is, in justice, about to be executed for the crime of treason; Immanuel is like a man who chooses to live a life sentence behind bars in place of a person who is guilty of killing a loved one of the very innocent man who is taking his place; or, as I have stated, the Savior is like the one who flies into a storm, risking his life to save those being pummeled by the elements of the very hurricane they have created.

And his love for us, and his willingness to cross over, do not end with the instantaneous moment of the incarnation. They continue into Jesus' public ministry in ways utterly astounding.

Jesus' Crossing Over in His Public Ministry

For those accustomed to the story of Jesus, and who regularly revisit these narratives as recorded in the Gospels, it is possible to domesticate the happenings of Jesus' life, and drain the strangeness from the drama.[46] The stories are read Sunday after Sunday, and they can become sterilized, washed clean of their radicality. Taking note of this possibility, in what follows, I invite readers to view the mysteries of Christ's public ministry through the lens of the theme of crossing over. What one comes to see, I think, are countless situations where Jesus rightly perceives the storm brewing on the horizon and walks determinedly toward it, crossing over into whatever awaits him.

---

46. See Robert Barron, *The Strangest Way: Walking the Christian Path* (Maryknoll: Orbis, 2004), especially at 9–10.

Take, for instance, when Jesus encounters the Gadarene Demoniacs, one of the many stories of Christ engaging those depicted as being possessed by demons.[47]

On the horizon lies a group of men who appear so hellish and obscene, that they can only be understood by the people of the time as demonically possessed. Word of these ghastly creatures is known throughout the area. They are out of control. Matthew describes them as being "so savage that no one could travel by that road" (8:28b). Luke depicts the possessed as unclothed and having broken free of chains and shackles (8:26-31). These men are dangerous and quite utterly grotesque. Most people, in the face of a possible encounter with these men, would chart a new path to avoid these ostracized individuals. Not Jesus. He moves right into their company with little regard for his own safety, allows them to approach, and does not shy away. He crosses over.

Or consider how Jesus responded in the face of the so-called 'sinners' of society. The calling of Matthew is a quintessential example (Mt. 9:9-13).

Imagine an outpost on the margins of a town. Men are relaxing. People are conversing. Gossip is flowing. If Jesus wanted to establish himself as a moral leader of his people in the usual fashion, he would probably have passed on by, or at least chosen not to converse with the shady characters at this post. What does Jesus do? He goes directly into the bustle, moves next to one of the more notorious figures, the tax collector, Matthew, the one likely despised by many of the people, and begins to address him. He doesn't

---

47. The character in this story is referred to in various ways, such as the Gadarene, Gerasene, or Gazarene demoniac. Also, depending on which Gospel is referred to, the number of demon-possessed men varies. For literary reasons, I refer to the demoniacs in the plural form.

just talk to him, which he does. He crosses right over to him and calls this sinner to be his disciple! And seemingly wanting to double down on his ministry of crossing over, Jesus deepens his intimacy with Matthew as they share a meal together—a meal!—in front of the naysayers. In this meal, which would foreshadow all *sacred meals* to follow, Jesus could barely have chosen a more important custom of his time to show his willingness to cross over to the rejected world.[48]

Then there is the example of Jesus crossing over to the leper (Mt. 8:1-4; Mk. 1:40-45). Before St. Damien, Jesus was (see chapter three).

Again, no one during Jesus' time understood leprosy, at least not to the extent that people do today. This disease was deadly in many ways, from the morbid loneliness of social isolation to the actual termination of a beating heart after a long and laborious struggle with infection.[49] Noting the seriousness of this and other skin diseases, the Jewish tradition that Jesus was a part of had proposed many practices for the community to follow (Lev. 13-14). In some cases, lepers were viewed as such a grave danger to those around them that they needed to dress a particular way and to announce their presence with shouts and gesticulation.

---

48. It is important to note here that I am not implying that Jesus willy-nilly offers an invitation to sinners to dine with him without inviting them to a new way of living—i.e., without inviting them to a conversion of sorts. What Jesus does after crossing over, and the theme of invitation, will be covered in the next chapter.

49. For a slightly different interpretation of this text, see Myrick C. Shinall, Jr., "The Social Condition of Lepers in the Gospels," *Journal of Biblical Literature* 137, no. 4 (2018): 915–934. It is beyond the purpose of this book to debate the social standing of lepers in Jesus' time, though this article is helpful in providing nuance.

What does Jesus do? Does he follow the usual customs and avoid the unsavory situation of encountering a leper? Nope. He crosses over. Not only does he remain in the presence of the leper, but he also reaches out his hand to touch the leper and to heal him! A more intimate example of engagement is difficult to find.

What about the people of Jesus' native town?

It is understandable that not everyone can go back home, and this seems to be most assuredly true for prophets, sages, and teachers. Jesus' tradition is replete with stories of those who did not fare well with their own people (Jer. 11:21-23; Ex. 2:11-15; Mt. 13:57). Any other town than his own native one would likely have produced a better audience than Nazareth. Most ordinary teachers or rabbis would choose the path of least resistance, moving away from the storm, seeking out more receptive audiences.

Not Jesus. Committed to crossing over, his mission was not ordinary.

To the people of his own town he returned, even though rejection seemed inevitable (Mk. 6:4). His visit to Nazareth was so alarming that his own people tried to throw him over a cliff (Lk. 4:16-30). (Now those are some wonderful relatives!) Nevertheless, Jesus did not shy away from deepening his incarnational movement.

And what about the mass of humanity that was sick, hungry, decrepit, suffering, homeless, obstinate, ill-intentioned, rejected, and forlorn? Jesus crossed over so as to heal the sick, feed the hungry, defend the defenseless, educate the ignorant, walk among the dispossessed, forgive the sinner, and provide hope to the hopeless. He made himself available to be touched, bothered, surrounded, accused, and nearly overwhelmed—he crossed over to give himself totally and completely into the storms forming around him.

Then came the moment in his life to approach the den of vipers living in Jerusalem: his encounter with some of the hypocritical leaders of the Jewish people, who would ultimately usher in Jesus' demise (Lk. 19:28-44). Jesus already had numerous contentious run-ins with some of these leaders (Jn. 2:13-25). There are whole chapters in the Gospels containing Jesus' recognition of the loathsome role some of these men played in Jewish life during Jesus' time (Mt. 23:1-39). When the *kairotic* moment arrived, rather than avoid these unpleasant souls, Jesus was resolutely determined to cross over into Jerusalem to encounter these leaders (Lk. 9:51). He did not back away despite the pleas from his friends, or the impending danger (Lk. 9:22; Mk. 8:31-33). He walked toward the storm as the hurricane intensified over Jerusalem where he would face two final moments of crossing over: the cross itself, and his impending descent to the realm of the dead.[50]

Crossing Over in His Passion and Death

The theology regarding Jesus' passion and death overflows with meaning, and it will not be possible here to capture fully the mystery of the *last things* in Jesus' life.[51] Nevertheless, I invite us, one last time, to put on the mind of Christ, and to dwell upon the storm to which Jesus would cross over following his entrance into Jerusalem.

---

50. I will be using the descent to the realm of the dead interchangeably with the descent into 'hell.' More on this will be covered below.

51. For one account of the last things, see Hans Urs von Balthasar, "Eschatology in Outline," in *Explorations in Theology IV: Spirit and Institution*, trans. Edward T. Oakes, S.J. (San Francisco: Ignatius, 1995), 423–467. See, also, Fleming Rutledge, *The Crucifixion: Understanding the Death of Jesus Christ* (Grand Rapids: Eerdmans, 2015).

Behold the cross. People growing up in the shadow of the Roman Empire knew of its cruelty. It was an instrument of a grotesque, public, degrading, and shameful death.[52] Its publicity existed as a warning to anyone considering a life of crime. It shouted to all: Beware the nails being pounded through flesh, the bones splintering, and the nerves splicing: this could be your flesh, your bones, and your nerves. People thought twice about their actions once they heard the cries on the multitudinous 'calvaries' throughout the empire. Horror would fill any who were aware of the asphyxiation induced under the weight of one's own body hanging from the tree of death for many agonizing hours, as birds of the air, and the eyes of onlookers, were tempted to feast on flesh not yet turned cold from the passing of one's soul. Jesus knew what this fate entailed.

What is more, however, the cross was not just a disgraceful and excruciatingly painful instrument of death. For Jesus, the cross meant something more. It would be the site of a cosmic drama—a *spiritual* battle—prefigured before the ages, where the Lamb of God would take upon himself the sin and suffering of the world (Jn. 1:29). The cross that presented itself to Jesus was not solely about physical and psychological pain; it meant enduring ontological pain and existential torment, where all the suffering, savagery, and sinfulness of the world would be placed on Christ as scapegoat, so that he might take away the sins of the world.[53]

---

52. See Rutledge, The Crucifixion, 72–84.
53. For more on the theme of 'the scapegoat,' see René Girard, The Scapegoat, trans. Yvonne Freccero (Baltimore: The Johns Hopkins University Press, 1986).

Balthasar, a theologian renown for his extensive reflections on the last things of Christ, captures the meaning of what crossing to the cross would entail for Jesus:

> In the suffering of the living Jesus, there is a readiness to drink the "chalice" of wrath, that is, to let the whole power of sin surge over him. He takes the blows, and the hate they express, upon himself and, as it were, amortizes it through his own suffering. The impotence of suffering (and the active readiness to undergo that impotence) outlasts every power of hammering sin. Sin's impatience, as the sum of all world-historical sinful impatience against God, is finally exhausted in comparison to the patience of the Son of God. His patience undergirds sin and lifts it off its hinges.[54]

In the old covenant, the ritual lamb was led to the ceremony unwillingly, and bore the sins of the people into the wilderness unknowingly. In the new sacrifice, the Lamb of God, fully aware of the fate that awaits him, crosses over by his own choice, willingly takes upon himself the full reality of the cross, walks the *via dolorosa*, and brings salvation to the world.[55]

As if this experience of the torments of hell being unleashed on his person while hanging on the cross was not already enough of a storm to endure—as if the Son of God needed to do even more to demonstrate his love for all—the *last things* for Christ included one final moment of crossing over: a movement to the realm of the dead.

After the physical, psychological, and ontological scandal of the suffering servant on the cross, Jesus hands

---

54. Hans Urs von Balthasar, "On Vicarious Representation," in *Explorations in Theology IV: Spirit and Institution*, trans. Edward T. Oakes, S.J. (San Francisco: Ignatius, 1995), 421.

55. Rutledge, *The Crucifixion*, 248–249.

over his spirit (Lk. 23:46). In this moment, he makes one final journey. As the Church professes in the Apostle's Creed, Christ descends into hell (1 Pet. 3:18-20).[56] He sees in the distance the gates of the place of darkness, the 'location' of those who have died prior to the event of the Savior, and moves toward those dark clouds. Christ is aware of the storm, and through a mysterious movement, in partnership with the Father and the Spirit, crosses over into the swirling tempests of those who have been abandoned into death. Though there is much mystery involved in this moment when "a great silence reigns on earth,"[57] something remarkable takes place. In the mystery of Jesus' death and descent to the realm of the dead, the Son of God now completes his mission of crossing over, as he journeys to the remotest peripheries to bring back what was lost. He walks right into hell to spring those who have been waiting in darkness.

Perhaps one of the most important theologians of the last hundred years, Joseph Ratzinger, writing during his early years as a professor of theology, captures the immense movement of crossing over witnessed to by Christ in his descent to hell. Ratzinger states:

> [In his descent to the realm of the dead, the Church professes that] Christ strode through the gate of

---

56. For more on this mystery of faith, see Joseph Ratzinger, *Introduction to Christianity*, trans. J.R. Foster and Michael J. Miller (San Francisco: Ignatius Press, 2004), 293–310. See, also, Hans Urs von Balthasar, *Theo-Drama V: Theological Dramatic Theory: The Last Act*, trans. Graham Harrison (San Francisco: Ignatius Press, 1998). See, also, Alyssa Lyra Pitstick, *Light in Darkness: Hans Urs von Balthasar and the Catholic Doctrine of Christ's Descent into Hell* (Grand Rapids: Eerdmans, 2007).

57. This quote is from an ancient Christian homily for Holy Saturday, and can be found in Catholic Church, *Catechism of the Catholic Church* (New York: Doubleday, 1995), no. 635.

our final loneliness...[In] his Passion he went down into the abyss of our abandonment. Where no voice can reach us any longer, there is he. Hell is thereby overcome, or, to be more accurate, death, which was previously hell, is hell no longer. Neither is the same any longer because there is life in the midst of death, because love dwells in it.[58]

Crossing over even to the furthest regions of Hades to encounter those who are far from the light of God, Jesus witnesses to his Church what it means to love, to be loved, and to live a mission of love in the world—not even the gates of hell impede the Son of God from crossing over to save the world.

The Church's Motivation

As I bring this chapter to close, I want to summarize where we have been by highlighting the motivation that exists for Christians to consider crossing over as essential to their life in Christ.

First, secular research indicates that crossing over is likely the most beneficial activity for overcoming some of the negative consequences of polarization. From a purely natural (as distinct from supernatural) perspective, the research into this subject should provide considerable impetus for those desiring to act in order to overcome some of the negative ramifications of polarization.

Furthermore, as I have shown, the mission of the Son of God was one thoroughly infused with the spirit of crossing over. Jesus' example should provide ample evidence that any Christian seriously dedicated to following Christ, and

---

58. Ratzinger, *Introduction to Christianity*, 299.

putting on 'his mind,' cannot help but feel called to engage in some manner of crossing over in his own missionary discipleship, to deepen Christ's incarnational movement in the world.[59]

Finally, when Christians realize that Christ underwent his mission of crossing over not just for the entire world in an abstract sense, but for everyone—for each individual—including each reader of this book, they realize that Jesus has accomplished something extraordinary for them personally. He entered into this world and embraced the storm in the various manifestations named above, because he loved each of us. In that love he has saved each of us.

He chose the incarnation for you and for me. He chose the leper for you and for me. He chose the sinner for you and for me. He chose the cross, and hell, for you and for me. He chose you, and he chose me.

As these grounds for motivation are pondered and appropriated, a subsequent question emerges: Now that I know I am called to cross over in my missionary discipleship, and as I see it is necessary in all eras, but especially in a polarized one, what do I do when I cross over into the storms of polarization, and encounter the other?

This question will be taken up in the following chapter.

---

59. Balthasar, *Razing the Bastions*, 71.

Chapter Six

Discipleship and Salvific Encounter

"How in the world did I get here?"

The turbulence is tremendous. The aircraft shudders, vibrates, and shakes as it barrels deeper into the hurricane. Clouds speed past. Light dims. Darkness thickens. Rain pours. It doesn't seem like the plane will hold together.

And then the shaking stops. Darkness dissipates. Blue brightens the background. Shuddering shifts to a quiet hum. And in a mesmerizing glimmer of hope and serenity, the sun appears like a comet on the horizon, a guiding star to passengers on the plane.

"In the eye of a hurricane there is quiet, for just a moment..."[1]

The scene above can be witnessed in a series of videos showcasing the aircraft fittingly named Hurricane Hunter traveling through Hurricane Florence.[2] The footage

---

1. See Lin-Manuel Miranda, "Hurricane," *Hamilton* (2015).
2. Nick Underwood, "What It's Like to Fly Through Hurricane Florence," *Popular Science*, September 12, 2018, https://www.youtube.com/watch?v=RUAn37OdfvE; NOAA, "Flying Through the Eye of Hurricane Florence," *Bloomberg Quicktake*, September 11, 2018, https://

stimulates the senses. Watching it creates the sensation of being on the plane, looking out a window, hearing the sounds, and feeling the intensity.

One hurricane hunter described flying into the eye of a storm like this: "As we approached the middle of the storm in the pitch black of morning, lightning momentarily lit up the sky and silhouetted the massive clouds we were getting ready to fly through, which would then vanish in the darkness just as quickly as they appeared. It was right after one of these flashes that I had the proverbial 'How in the world did I get here?' moment."[3]

How, indeed?

It turns out that hurricane hunters 'get to the eye,' because that is their goal. It is not enough just to be in the hurricane. They must fly into the eye, for it provides some of the most important data that facilitates measuring the intensity of the storm and mapping its possible trajectory.[4]

So that a crew of storm chasers can succeed, their aircraft is loaded with navigation devices. The real time data collected is compared to what was known about the storm, and the crew constantly analyzes the information they have obtained, reworks calculations, and adjusts their course as needed.

As one professional storm chaser stated: "[Though] we go into each storm armed with the best available information about the conditions we should encounter, the

www.youtube.com/watch?v=oTiTd9RCG5A; https://www.youtube.com/watch?v=54jyDX9bLVU; NOAA, "Here's What It Looks Like to Fly Directly Into the Eye of Hurricane Florence," *Time*, September 11, 2018, https://www.youtube.com/watch?v=wEzeOWKuESo.

3.   See National Weather Service: National Oceanic and Atmospheric Administration, "Flying Through the Eye of the Storm: NOAA Hurricane Hunters," n.d., https://www.weather.gov/wrn/hurricane_hunter.

4.   See National Weather Service, "Flying Through the Eye."

dynamic nature of the environment means the only sure things about your trip are the bumps behind you." He humbly confesses: "I have an immense respect for every storm we approach."[5]

The previous chapter of this book was an invitation to readers to consider 'crossing over' into the storms of the contemporary polarized milieu. This chapter seeks to provide some of the 'equipment' or 'tools' to navigate the storms into which people have chosen to cross. As will be shown, each of these 'tools' can be witnessed in Jesus' own ministry of crossing over. Their utility is also based on current literature addressing the science of polarization.

Though not an exhaustive list of what is required by those who choose to cross over, I propose three tools that can assist people in navigating the polarized hurricanes of today. They are: 1) flexibility; 2) curiosity; and 3) prudence.

Before describing each of these tools, a few words need to be said about what goal Christians should consider pursuing after crossing over into a polarized hurricane.[6]

Salvific Encounter as the Eye of the Storm

What is the 'eye of the storm,' i.e., the goal, that should be the target of any mission of crossing over? To answer this question, I invite us to look, once again, to the witness of Jesus and to the second of the two main aspects of his incarnational movement: *salvific encounter*.

After the Son of God crossed over into creation through the incarnation, his singular focus was the salva-

---

5. See National Weather Service, "Flying Through the Eye."
6. On the importance of having a general goal in mind when addressing the challenge of polarization, see Coleman, *The Way Out*, 190–203. See, also, Lee, *Talking Across*, 40–41.

tion of the world. As recorded in the Gospel of John, Jesus states: "I came so that they might have life and have it more abundantly" (Jn. 10:10b). Jesus' movement to accomplish this goal would culminate, as I explored in the previous chapter, in the cross and through the resurrection, as the universal cosmic drama of salvation played out.

Perhaps counterintuitively, however, Jesus' ministry of salvation, though universal, was decorated with countless intimate moments of *salvific encounter*. Not only did he cross over to those around him. He also *encountered* individuals or small groups along the journey in order to provide a *salvific* offering to them, which would anticipate the fullness of salvation he desired for all.

These moments of salvific encounter had a similar pattern. He met individuals or small groups, came to know them and their needs, listened to them and asked questions, shared with them some of his own stories and thoughts, and then imparted to them whatever they seemed to desire in that moment, or whatever he discerned was needed.[7] To the woman suffering from bleeding, he shared healing (Mk. 5:25-34). To those who struggled to believe, he offered faith (Jn. 20:24-29). To the hypocritical, he provided a correction (Mt. 23). And to countless people, he shared his teachings (e.g., Mt. 5-6).

In imitation of Jesus, Christians, once crossing over into the polarized storms of life, will need to seek out the eye of the storm, i.e., if they desire to imitate Jesus, they will need to seek out moments of salvific encounter. This means that when Christians conduct their mission, they are seeking the **right conditions** such that there can be a

---

7.   For an exploration of aspects of the ministry of Jesus, see James Martin, SJ, *Building a Bridge: How the Catholic Church and the LGBT Community Can Enter into a Relationship of Respect, Compassion, and Sensitivity* (New York: HarperOne, 2018), especially 67–75.

mutual exchange between them and those they engage. This mutual exchange will often include **dialogue** where both parties **speak** and are **heard**, along with the sharing of various types of **gifts**, from personal stories, wisdom, truths about reality, opinions about the present state of the world, or acts of love and kindness. All this is ordered toward a situation where all parties involved grow in **communion** together, and with God.

No doubt, these are weighty theological statements. The contours of 'salvific encounter' will be elaborated upon further throughout the remainder of this chapter as I suggest 'tools' for pursuing these experiences. For the present discussion, however, a concrete example is appropriate to help illuminate what I am describing.

Salvific Encounters through a Ministry of Presence

I belong to a Catholic missionary religious order, the Glenmary Home Missioners, which serves rural counties of the United States in the southeast and Appalachia. Glenmary priests, brothers, sisters, and lay people conduct their mission in predominantly non-Catholic (less than one percent) and economically poor areas by seeking to instantiate more deeply the reality of the Church, often including building up the parish structure; by fostering relationships with the people of the area; and by collaborating with the local community, especially non-Catholic Christians, for the salvific benefit of all.[8]

---

8. It should be noted that my reference to 'salvific' here implies a theology of 'integral' salvation. For more on the various theological themes contained in this section, see Stephen B. Bevans and Roger P. Schroeder, *Prophetic Dialogue: Reflections on Christian Mission To-*

Throughout much of Glenmary's history, including today, many members have sought salvific encounters through what is often called a 'ministry of presence.' Through this ministry, the missioners pursue the **right conditions** for salvific encounters by habitually 'crossing over' to a commonly frequented social setting in the community. At these places, they make themselves available to those who desire to engage them. For instance, they might enter a fast-food establishment or rest stop, order a coffee, and remain there for hours. In general, the missioners have little immediate agenda beyond wanting to meet the people, and to follow where the grace and Spirit of God guide them.

As they are present to the people in these locations, there begins to occur various forms of **mutual exchange**. With some people, they just smile, wave, or make some gesture or greeting. These gestures may also accompany sharing the **gifts** of simple pleasantries, noting the weather, the crops, the outcome of the local football game, or other information. Though small, these exchanges are not unimportant, as they serve to establish the foundation of relationships that lend themselves to deeper conversations.[9]

With some of the people they come across, the missioners often begin casual conversations or **dialogues**, which vary in content based on the **conditions presenting themselves**, e.g., what the person is interested in, how often the missioners have spoken with the person, the nature of their relationship, the emotional readiness of the person, or how much time is available. Far from being

---

day (Maryknoll: Orbis, 2011).

9.   On the importance of these more mundane pleasantries, see Chesterton, *What's Wrong*. Chesterton addresses this theme in chapter thirteen, titled "Wisdom and the Weather."

a weak or ineffectual approach to ministry, this dialogue, in ways harmonizing current research on polarization,[10] tends toward meaningful conversations where hearts are opened, and begin to change.[11]

From the dialogue, some people they encounter begin to ask the missioners interesting questions. "Why are you here?" "What is your occupation?" "Do you belong to a local church?" "Do you have a family?" These basic questions often turn to deeper sharing about life, love, meaning, politics, and even God, and promote opportunities for the missioners to ask questions of their own. Over time, some of the conversations become regular fixtures in people's lives, almost like ongoing spiritual direction. More than a few of the exchanges even include deeper expressions of **communion**, such as prayer, words of mutual gratitude, the sharing of resources with a person in need, or an invitation to worship together on the weekend.

What is more, many of the encounters these missioners have with the people lead to their own (the missioners') increased **communion** with the local community, as they are invited to join, or participate in, existing groups or organizations that work toward building up the local community. This can include participation in the civic life of the community, service on local boards, or volunteering with nonprofit organizations. These invitations, when answered, only continue to enrich the missioners' experience in the area, as well as the lives of those they encounter. In this way and others, the missioners receive

---

10. See, for instance, Lee, *Talking Across*, 23–37. See, also, Coleman, *The Way Out*, 9–13.

11. On this point, see Pope Francis and Austin Ivereigh, *Let Us Dream: The Path to a Better Future* (New York: Simon and Schuster, 2020)

from those they encounter, such that the salvific moment is **mutually enriching**.

Now, there needs to be full disclosure here. The missioners bring to these moments their own limitations, and they do not always respond with grace and charity to those they encounter. Moreover, not everyone desires to talk to the missioners. Some people are outright hostile once engaged. When these situations arise, the missioners seek to employ the tools I will discuss below, from remaining flexible, to continuing to be curious, to deciding, in prudence, to walk away. And yet, even these more hostile exchanges can be moments of grace if the missioners involved approach them wisely. Many people, after seeking to argue with the missioners, return more open to dialogue.

It might be the case that readers are wondering: I can see how these are legitimate 'encounters' between different people, but what makes these encounters 'salvific?' To be sure, only God knows to what extent grace, and by consequence, salvation, is or is not operative in any of these situations. However, Christians are called to "collaborate in the salvation of others" by being channels of grace in the world.[12] This takes on a more formal manifestation in the Sacraments of the Church, where God works through people in specific ways to channel grace in the world. But there are numerous human interactions that can be considered 'sacramental,' in which people serve as the conduits of grace for others. Many of the examples shared above in the life of Glenmary led to quite explicit moments where grace seemed to be present, such as sharing prayer, conversations about faith and the church, and even worship.

---

12. See Catholic Church, *Catechism*, no. 2003.

Moreover, in the exchanges that are not explicitly dealing with issues related to faith, grace can be both operative, and preparing those involved for something more.[13] Christians who facilitate salvific encounters can trust that any interaction that involves the exchange of truth, goodness, or beauty, whether in conversation or through a loving gesture or action, can move those involved ever so slightly into deeper communion with the God who is Truth, Goodness, and Beauty.[14] Missioners who cross over are concerned with multiplying these positive exchanges of grace around them, always seeking to assist people in responding more fully to the grace of Christ in and through the Church.[15]

From what I have described, seeking out salvific encounters can be an arduous though rewarding task, and one that, especially in a polarized age, can be rife with challenges. What is more, not everyone will have the freedom, for example, to 'hang around' McDonald's for three hours a day. Neither will everyone have the character or talent to do so (this requires a certain extroversion and courage). This is understandable, and I am not arguing that visiting McDonald's must be the way all people should approach missionary discipleship.[16] There are a plethora of options for crossing over and facilitating salvific encounters in the contemporary period (many examples will be provided in the last chapter). Nevertheless, all Christians concerned with missionary discipleship should be challenged, in

---

13. For a classic novel that highlights this point, see Georges Bernanos, *The Diary of a Country Priest* (Boston: Da Capo Press, 2002).

14. On this point, see Soujeole, *Introduction to the Mystery*, 247–268.

15. For more on the theology of 'communion,' see Joseph Cardinal Ratzinger, *Called to Communion: Understanding the Church Today*, trans. Adrian Walker (San Francisco: Ignatius, 1996), 21–29.

16. On this type of activity, see Chris Arnade, *Dignity: Seeking Respect in Back Row America* (New York: Sentinel, 2019).

imitation of Jesus, to find ways to cross over and pursue salvific encounters.

To aid this process, a cultivation of the use of particular 'tools' becomes necessary. It is to the first of these tools, 'flexibility,' that I now turn.

Flexibility in the Storm

To facilitate moments of salvific encounter, Christians will benefit from cultivating flexibility in their lives. By flexibility, I mean one's ability to adapt freely and spontaneously to the complex situations and people that are present when one approaches others in a ministry of crossing over.[17] To highlight the nature, and importance, of flexibility, I showcase the example Jesus.

The Flexibility of Jesus in His Ministry

Jesus adapted freely to the multiplicity of people and situations in his public ministry. In chapter five, I explored some of the diverse situations he encountered. Among others, he engaged lepers, demoniacs, the sick, the lame, the hypocritical, the critical, those who loved him, those who hated him, those who betrayed him, massive crowds, claustrophobic gatherings, inhospitable townspeople, pagans, those who sought to do him harm, those labeled sinners, those who sought ceremonial holiness, and more. The inherent logic of Christ's crossing over was ordered to the encounter of complex situations and people. Though

---

17. On the importance of 'adaptive' or 'flexible' leadership in the contemporary period, see Tod Bolsinger, *Canoeing the Mountains: Christian Leadership in Unchartered Territory* (Downers Grove: IVP Books, 2018), 32–44.

it might be assumed that Jesus responded in the same way to the people he encountered, a close look at his ministry reveals that he was able to adapt to the many situations he encountered and respond in just as many ways.

In some cases, Jesus asked questions, and listened with an extraordinarily open ear. For instance, when he encountered the man born blind (Mk. 10:46-52), the woman caught in adultery and her accusers (Jn. 8:1-11), or his disciples throughout various moments of his life (e.g., Mt. 16: 13-23; Jn. 21:15-17), he inquired into their perspectives, and listened attentively and with patience, to their concerns.[18] (I will have much more to say on this theme in the following section.)

In other situations, Jesus assumed the role of teacher. This is famously observed in the Sermon on the Mount (Mt. 5), or in the robust dialogue Jesus held with Nicodemus (Jn. 3). Whether addressing individuals or crowds of varying sizes, Jesus, as teacher, imparted wisdom to others.

With certain people, Jesus was argumentative, even polemical, using his knowledge and learning to debate and defend the message his Father had given to him (cf. Mt. 21:12-13; Mk. 3:1-5). Often, though not exclusively, these moments arose when, motivated by what appeared to be righteous indignation, he 'strongly encouraged' the scribes, Pharisees, and others, to a conversion of heart (Mt. 23). In many of these instances, Jesus did not mince words and directly, though lovingly, challenged people to *metanoia*, or a conversion of life.

In other scenarios that called for it, Jesus told stories, providing parables rich with meaning. From the Lost Sheep (Mt. 18:10-14), to the Prodigal Son (Lk. 15:11-32), and to countless other parables, the recounting of these evoca-

---

18. Tom Hughes, *Curious: The Unexpected Power of a Question-Led Life* (Bonita Springs: NavPress, 2015).

tive narratives seemed to be one of Jesus' preferred mediums when attempting to communicate difficult truths.

At other times, particularly toward the end of his life, Jesus was silent, even when it seemed talking would be beneficial (e.g., Lk. 23:9; Mt. 26:63; cf. Is. 53:7). In the face of his accusers, the Son of Man let silence be his defense.

The above list is not exhaustive. The important point to consider here is that Jesus was far from predictable in his response to those around him. He surveyed the situation, sought to understand the conditions presented to him, listened to his audience, and responded with flexibility by adapting to the information, people, and situations he encountered. At times, he was thoroughly compassionate and open, at other times, he responded with righteous anger. At times he was bold, stood his ground, or performed life-altering miracles, at others, he walked away, or willingly handed over his life.

Those who want to model Jesus' ministry will benefit from noting the diversity of responses he utilized to the various situations he encountered. Like Jesus, his followers who choose to cross over to cultivate salvific moments should seek to remain flexible to the conditions that present themselves. If Christians approach the polarized world which exists today thoroughly convinced that they need to respond in singular, narrow ways, it will likely be the case that their facilitation of salvific moments will be limited.

Harmonizing with the example of Jesus, contemporary research on polarization points to the importance of flexibility as well.

Flexibility and the Science of Polarization

Current research on the science of polarization affirms the value of maintaining flexibility while crossing over into polarized groups, so that one is able to adapt to the multitudinous people and situations one may encounter. Flexibility through adaptability becomes particularly helpful in instances where tense conversations occur around intractable, contentious issues that are not likely to resolve themselves in a short period of time.[19] In these situations involving 'intractable landscapes,' flexibility tends to produce more meaningful exchanges. As Peter T. Coleman and his colleagues discovered in their research at the Difficult Conversations Lab at Columbia University: "The best results, or the results that lead to more constructive engagement and more sustainable solutions over time, are those that result from a process of adaptation to the inevitable changes in the [engagement of contentious issues and situations]."[20]

Coleman and his colleagues found, for instance, that flexibility in people's *response* to the other while engaging in difficult conversations, meaning that people are more open to responding in a variety of ways to their interlocutor, rather than responding in singular, rigid, and predetermined ways, resulted in longer and more meaningful engagements.[21] Furthermore, when people were more flexible with integrating various *perspectives* on contentious issues, meaning that they were open to listen to, consider, and integrate a variety of sources and opinions into their own personal perspectives, they were more likely to have successful conversations that reached mutually beneficial compromises.[22] Finally, among other research from Coleman and his colleagues, the more flexible one

---

19. For more on 'intractable' issues, see Coleman, *The Way Out*, 47–58.
20. Coleman, *The Way Out*, 203.
21. See Coleman, *The Way Out*, 39; 50–58; 67–80; 193.
22. Coleman, *The Way Out*, 192–195.

was regarding a desired *outcome* from an exchange with an out-group other, the more likely a person was to have long-term engagements that changed hearts and promoted the exchange of rich ideas and information.[23]

Other research on polarization suggests that if people enter a situation of crossing over and presume they know, with certainty, the positions of their interlocutor, generalize about the other person's perspective, simplify the solution to complex problems, or fail to engage the nuance and complexity of another's perspective, it will likely be the case that people are not going to facilitate a situation where dialogue and mutual exchange are possible.[24] In contradistinction to these approaches of engagement, the one who is more open (flexible) to the complexity of an issue, seeks to understand and learn the nuances of a person's perspective, and does not make assumptions about what the other person is going to say regarding a particular issue, is more likely to have meaningful exchanges where genuine dialogue occurs.[25]

Given the importance of flexibility in today's polarized milieu, it is important to consider how to cultivate flexibility in one's life.

---

23. Coleman, in his work on polarization, notes four areas of 'flexibility' that can enhance exchanges around contentious issues: 1) tolerance for ambiguity; 2) cognitive complexity; 3) emotional complexity; and 4) behavioral complexity. See *The Way Out*, 190–195. On the research regarding the importance of adapting to complex situations, and the detrimental effect of 'rigidity,' see, for instance, Coleman, *The Way Out*, 39; 50–58; 67–80. See, also, Jacobs, *How to Think*, 125–138. See, also, Grant, *Think Again*, 102–116.
24. See Coleman, *The Way Out*, 138–160. See, also, Lee, *Talking Across*, 49–60.
25. See Guzmán, *I Never Thought*, 137–140.

Cultivating Flexibility

The cultivation of flexibility requires one to answer the invitation of the famous Oracle at Delphi to "Know oneself."[26] Research around polarization indicates that flexibility in responding to polarized situations can be cultivated by asking meaningful questions of oneself and reflecting on one's own personal perspectives, feelings, expectations, and priorities in relationship to those questions, *prior* to seeking to facilitate moments of encounter. In other words, it seems to be the case that the more one is aware of one's ideas, feelings, and expectations, the more one can be attentive to others and subsequently respond in a manner that can bring about meaningful exchanges.[27]

As documented in his book *The Way Out: How to Overcome Toxic Polarization*, Coleman's research suggests that a consideration of a variety of questions about oneself can assist a person in preparing to navigate the challenges of polarization and, depending on one's perspectives, can aid flexibility. For instance, Coleman notes that people should reflect upon their personal theory of change (i.e., whether they think people can actually change at all),[28] their personal emotional state prior to conversing with

---

26. On the importance of this theme, see Hans Urs von Balthasar, *Theo-Drama: Theological Dramatic Theory I: Prolegomena*, trans. Graham Harrison (San Francisco: Ignatius, 1988), 481–491.

27. Though I am utilizing social scientific research on polarization to highlight this point, there exists research in the area of psychology that resonates with these findings. See John Mark Falkenhain, *How We Love: A Formation for the Celibate Life* (Collegeville: Liturgical Press, 2019), especially at 135–152.

28. See Coleman, *The Way Out*, 63–80; 98–101. As Coleman notes, actually believing that people might change can positively affect a polarized conversation.

others,[29] their preferred outcomes regarding an encounter in polarized situations (i.e., the goals or intentions they have in mind for the encounter),[30] and their preferred method of response in certain situations where contentious issues arise (e.g., fight, flight, fix, etc.).[31] To be sure, how one answers these questions, and how one integrates those answers into her life, matter for further cultivation of flexibility. Indeed, Coleman's book seeks to guide readers through these considerations in ways that bring about adaptability.[32] Nevertheless, it is enough to note that, according to Coleman, a first step to the cultivation of flexibility is to consider these, and other, questions about oneself.[33]

Additional research on issues related to polarization proposes that people need to ask questions regarding their own perspectives about polarized themes, and whether they think their interlocutors, especially those they disagree with, can enhance their own understanding through their disagreements.[34] Research suggests that, on the one hand, people who discern through reflection that their perspective is limited (i.e., that no matter how informed they are, they can still learn more) will more likely search out a variety of sources and people to help deepen their understanding and knowledge of a topic. They seem to be far more likely to admit their limitations and to rethink their ideas with the help of others.[35] On the other hand,

---

29. Coleman, *The Way Out*, 103–105.
30. See Coleman, *The Way Out*, 101–103.
31. See Coleman, *The Way Out*, 63–72.
32. For a summary of how one can be guided through some of these themes, see *The Way Out*, 200–217.
33. Coleman, *The Way Out*, 192–195; 200–203.
34. On this point, see Grant, *Think Again*, 52–53; 77–93.
35. Grant, *Think Again*, 65–70.

people who, through reflection, come to appreciate and desire the input of others, even if they disagree with them, will likely remain in conversation with those to whom they disagree, and entertain more meaningful, extended exchanges, when fraught disagreements arise.[36] In other words, when engaging in polarized storms, the quality of encounter depends on whether one has respect for the perspectives, and the input, of others with whom they disagree.

Finally, flexibility can be cultivated by reflecting on the complexity of other people's perspectives.[37] To grow in this area of flexibility, people should consider whether, and to what extent, they understand that their interlocutors likely form their positions and perspectives within a culturally contextualized personal history, such that the positions they maintain are always already interconnected to their personal story, their background, how they feel (not just what they think), and what they, personally, are experiencing at the present moment of their life (e.g., a strong position in favor of abortion can be influenced by a (recent) traumatic sexual experience).[38] Put simply, people do not think in a vacuum. Their ideas are complexly related to their entire lives.[39] People who accept the complexity of others and their perspectives are more likely to respond to the people in front of them in their complexity, especially in their personal story,[40] rather than simply and narrowly

---

36. See Grant, *Think Again*, 55–93.
37. Coleman, *The Way Out*, 138–160.
38. See, also, Lee, *Talking Across*, 63–81.
39. See Klein, *Why We're Polarized*, 98–102; 158–163; 261–264.
40. On the importance of listening to people's personal stories, see Lee, *Talking Across*, 63–81.

attending to the presenting contentious issues alone and in isolation from broader considerations.[41]

Once people better realize and accept the complexity of the perspectives of the 'other' and the perspectives they hold, they can become more motivated to learn about those perspectives and people. To ensure that this pursuit is meaningfully fulfilled, the second 'tool' for navigating the storms of polarization is required: 'curiosity.'

Curiosity in the Storm

One main recommendation for navigating a polarized milieu in a meaningful way pervades research on polarization: Remain curious.[42] In as much as flexibility requires reflecting on one's self, looking inward in order to adapt outwardly in relationship to the other, curiosity motivates one to move outward, to the other and the other's world—including ideas, thoughts, and feelings. Through curiosity, one seeks to know and learn as much about the other as possible, never settling for easy, simplified explanations or answers, all the while remaining open to learning about oneself in the process of the mutual exchange. As the introspection necessary for flexibility moves one to unravel the mystery of the self, curiosity motivates one to unravel the mystery of the 'other,' such that, to a certain extent,

---

41. For instance, Coleman suggests a practice of 'radical relandscaping,' which is the process of seeking to understand the complexity around contentious themes by focusing not on the presenting problem, but on the context around the problem. See *The Way Out*, 73–74. See, also, Guzmán, *I Never Thought*, 46–47.

42. See Guzmán, *I Never Thought*, 49–71. See, also, Holland and Silvers, *I Think You're Wrong*, 103–115. See Lee, *Talking Across*, 49–60.

they no longer are 'other,' but are known more completely and truthfully.[43]

Sarah Stewart Holland and Beth Silvers, in their book about how they have sought to engage polarized culture, define genuine curiosity as follows:

> Seeking out facts, valuing data and expertise, and relentlessly asking questions—all questions: questions about one another's lives, questions about our perspectives both shared and unique, questions about our philosophies, why-are-we-here kinds of questions—these are pursuits that will help us examine ideas, issues, people, and our own beliefs clearly.[44]

Their definition is helpful, and points in the direction of what is often pursued by curious people: The curious person is a lover and pursuer of wisdom, seeking to plumb the depths of what is true, beautiful, and good in the world and, especially, in the person who one is engaging.[45] With a longing to know and understand, the curious person seeks the interconnectedness of all things, aspiring, in humility, to be granted insight into reality, all the while being convinced that others can assist them in the process.[46]

If there was a person who embodied curiosity by his willingness to ask many questions of those around him, it was Jesus.[47] It is to his example that I now turn.

---

43. See Jacobs, *How to Think*, 83.
44. *I Think You're Wrong*, 104.
45. Alberto Manguel, *Curiosity* (New Haven: Yale University Press, 2015), 11–29.
46. See Denis Robinson, "Everything That Rises Must Converge: Spiritual Direction and Literature," in *A Science of the Saints: Studies in Spiritual Direction*, ed. Robert E. Alvis (Collegeville: Liturgical Press, 2020), 195–213.
47. No doubt there exist other historical figures who epitomized the curious life, such as Socrates (c. 399), Leonardo Da Vinci (1452–1519),

The Curiosity of Jesus in His Ministry

Jesus asked a lot of questions. As referred to above, it was one of his main styles of engagement. Even though he was full of wisdom himself (cf. Lk. 2:40), he nevertheless desired to know other people's perspectives in and through their own words, thoughts, stories, feelings, and questions. He relentlessly asked questions of those around him, and listened attentively to their answers.

In his book *Curious: The Unexpected Power of a Question-Led Life*, Christian pastor and author Tom Hughes notes that asking questions was an integral part of Jesus' ministry. He states:

> Jesus did not hold many question-and-answer sessions. More often he held question-and-question sessions. His response to a question was often simply another question. Throughout the four Gospels of Jesus, he is asked 183 questions. Of those 183 questions, how many do you think he answered directly? Four. He responds to the other 179 questions with a question, a parable, or a cryptic remark that leaves those gathered with even more questions.[48]

Looking at a few of these 'question moments' of Jesus reveals insights into how curiosity can facilitate salvific encounters.

Jesus truly desired to know what people wanted, and he sought to allow them to articulate their desires. For

---

or Edith Stein (1891–1942), to name a few. For more on the theme of curiosity in relationship to evangelization and the ministry of Jesus, see Sherry A. Weddell, *Forming Intentional Disciples: The Path to Knowing and Following Jesus* (Huntington: Our Sunday Visitor, 2012), especially 141–154.

48. See Hughes, *Curious*, 4–5.

example, when the blind Bartimaeus approached, Jesus likely would have known very clearly what Bartimaeus was seeking (Mk. 10:46-52). The man was blind and would have presented that way, as years of poverty would have taken their toll. Most people likely would have assumed that Bartimaeus wanted to see. Not Jesus.

Instead of presuming upon his interlocutor, Jesus asked him a question: "What do you want me to do for you?" By allowing Bartimaeus to answer, a mutual exchange deeper than just the reception of healing materialized. Jesus, and likely the crowd around him, received the opportunity to observe the profound faith of a man whose life had been reduced to begging. Bartimaeus, for his part, not only received healing, he was given the chance to speak, to be heard, and to have his dignity affirmed.

Jesus also used his questions to elicit conversations around some of the most important truths about life. For instance, his question to his disciples, "But who do you say that I am?" is an inquiry into the profoundest mysteries of existence and faith. Through this question, Jesus is asking what his disciples think concerning his identity, his Father, the mystery of creation, and the path toward salvation down which Jesus was directing them (cf. Mt. 16:13-20).[49]

Even when Jesus' life was being threatened, when the storms of his time intensified around him, he maintained his posture of curiosity (Jn. 18:19-24). To the chief priests who were plotting to put Jesus to death, he asked, "Why ask me?" as a way to uncover what they believed about him and his Father. He further inquired: "[If] I have spoken rightly, why do you strike me?" Jesus was attempting, at a moment that was far from convenient, to help his antagonists think

---

49. See Hughes, *Curious*, 26–29.

about their perspectives and opinions, articulate them, if they were able, and demonstrate their 'true colors.'

Finally, among other examples, Jesus' questions, following his resurrection, demonstrated his desire to elicit wisdom. In Jesus' final moments of life leading up to his crucifixion, his disciples were quite pitiful. Some betrayed him. Others slept. Some failed to be at his side when he needed them most. For all intents and purposes, most of his disciples basically ceased being his followers. They fled the scene as their teacher was crucified. But their ill-treatment of Jesus before the crucifixion did not limit Jesus' ability after the resurrection to approach them with curiosity.[50]

After the resurrection, Jesus returned to his disciples. As if knowing they were ashamed on account of their pre-resurrection decisions, he asked them basic inquiries to reestablish the relationship. Had they caught any fish (cf. Jn. 21:5)? Did they have any food (cf. Lk. 24:41)? What were they conversing about (cf. Lk. 24:17)? He transcended their sheepish behavior with pleasantries, in order to pursue an exchange of wisdom, that is, the pursuit of the truth of who he really was, and to what his disciples were *still* being called. These moments approach a *dénouement* in Jesus' tripartite examination of Peter, which touched on the importance of love, forgiveness, and, ultimately, the very purpose and meaning of life (Jn. 21:15-19). "Do you love me?" was a question for the ages. In questioning Peter, Jesus questioned the world.

Clearly, Jesus asked a lot of questions. These queries elicited further questions, helped communicate difficult truths, surfaced the perspectives of those he engaged, and oftentimes allowed his interlocutors to touch more inti-

---

50. See Hughes, *Curious*, 41–45.

mately the truth, goodness, and beauty of life. Questions were used by Jesus to facilitate salvific moments.

Those who want to follow Jesus' example by remaining curious so as to facilitate salvific encounters should note the thoroughly curious nature of Jesus. Even as he is the Son of God and, therefore, blessed with divine foreknowledge, he shows that curiosity remains crucial to engaging the other. Even in difficult or contentious situations, when his own life was in jeopardy, he witnessed to the importance of curiosity.

Beyond the example of Jesus, much research on overcoming the challenges of polarization demonstrates that curiosity is a tool that can assist those attempting to navigate a polarized world.

Curiosity and the Science of Polarization

The literature about polarization shows that a polarized culture tends to produce the opposite of curiosity. Polarization tends to narrow vision and idolize certainty.[51]

One of the main challenges of living in a polarized world is that, rather than seeking wisdom by seeing the interconnectedness of all things, especially in the perspectives of the out-group, people tend to narrow their vision, oversimplify complex problems, categorize their interlocutors into easily manageable 'pigeonholes,' and even avoid the 'other' altogether, in the desire to arrange neatly their personal worldview.[52] Supported by much social psychological research, those who study polarization have noted that polarized culture tends to reinforce what is known as

---

51. Guzmán, I Never Thought, 54; 138.
52. See Guzmán, I Never Thought, 69–70.

the 'consistency principle,' i.e., that people have a strong urge primarily, if not exclusively, to engage with sources, people, and situations that confirm their narrative and vision of the world. Much like the cognitive biases explored in chapter three, the meaning behind the consistency principle, as a psychological concept, suggests that people are more likely to have an aversion to those things which do not affirm their vision—they are likely to avoid them, and they are likely only to consult sources that reinforce their perspective.[53]

Many people who have researched the problem of polarization recommend curiosity as an antidote to some of the tendencies inherent in the consistency principle.[54] Curiosity invites one to break away from overly simplistic narratives, and to eschew one-sided, narrow perspectives about other people. Curiosity invites one to ask questions, to explore, to admit limitations, and to desire the knowledge, experience, and stories of others so as to assist one in discovering the very mysteries of the world. The curious person longs for complexity, rejects an oversimplification of the world, and waits patiently with the discomfort of paradoxes and contradictory experiences.[55] The curious person transforms discomfort into more questions, and, in turn, further wisdom.

Being that curiosity is vitally important in navigating a polarized world, it is necessary to explore how one can cultivate this tool.

---

53. See Guzmán, I Never Thought, 42–43. See, also, Coleman, The Way Out, 19; 59.
54. Guzmán, I Never Thought, 49–97. See, also, Holland and Silvers, I Think You're Wrong, 103–115. See, also, Lee, Talking Across, 38–81.
55. Coleman, The Way Out, 135–160.

Cultivating Curiosity

A lot of research has been written on the cultivation of curiosity. Ian Leslie, for instance, in his book *Curious: The Desire to Know and Why Your Future Depends on It*, cites seven different ways for people to remain curious, from 'staying foolish' to 'foraging like a foxhog.'[56] These recommendations, along with others, are helpful in infusing the soul with curiosity.

For my purposes here, however, I want to reach back to the research of Mónica Guzmán in her book subtitled *How to Have Fearlessly Curious Conversations in a Dangerously Divided Time*. Her writing is, among other things, quite applicable to those who decide to cross over, who want to facilitate salvific moments, and who desire to do so by remaining curious even in the midst of the storm. Her research points to two considerations that are especially pertinent.

First, Guzmán notes that one step on the path to cultivating curiosity is to be aware of situations where people feel their own perspective being challenged, changed, or even shattered.[57] Whether in reading an article that presents a counternarrative to their view of the world, or when engaging the out-group other and listening to a perspective that is not people's own, there will inevitably arise moments where people begin to feel cognitive dissonance, where their mind begins to whirl, their stomach begins to sour, their blood pressure rises, or their heart beats faster. These moments of 'friction' are likely going to occur when one has chosen to cross over to engage the out-group oth-

---

56. See Ian Leslie, *Curious: The Desire to Know and Why Your Future Depends on It* (New York: Basic Books, 2014), 135–184.

57. See Guzmán, *I Never Thought*, 49–71.

er.[58] Guzmán recommends that people, especially those who desire to be curious, welcome these moments. They are, according to her, an important experience for the curious person. They can serve as a signal to people that they are likely on the verge of discovery. Something does not make sense, and it is important to find out why.

So that the curious discovery can be made, coupled with these moments must be the right response. Because of some of the consequences of living in a polarized world, people will likely, in these moments of friction, be tempted to reject, ignore, or cancel whatever seems to be 'rubbing them the wrong way.' However, in this moment, Guzmán invites people to respond, not with anger, hostility, aversion, or the closing of one's mind, but with a question. People, according to Guzmán, should train themselves, in these moments of discomfort, confusion, and even anger, to ask a curious question.

For instance, Guzmán admits that she enjoys the question "What am I missing?"[59] At the heart of this question is an openness to discovering what about a person's personal perspective, and about what the interlocutor is saying, are making the person uncomfortable. This question admits that there is something here, in this moment, which needs to be learned—some treasure waiting to be unearthed—to which one needs to remain open. This question, "What am I missing?" can be followed by a whole series of other, open-ended questions directed toward the interlocutor: "Can you tell me more?" "I have never thought of it that way. Please say more?" "Can you help me to understand what you are saying?" This last question is particularly useful, as one admits that it is oneself who

---

58. For more on 'friction,' see Guzmán, *I Never Thought*, 61–63.
59. Guzmán, *I Never Thought*, 49–50.

needs assistance in understanding, and not necessarily the other person who is deficient.[60]

To be sure, these two basic considerations for engaging the out-group other will not guarantee a salvific encounter, but they certainly have the potential to allow curiosity to reign in the pursuit of salvific moments. Sometimes attending to these very practical matters can provide the environment in which wisdom is discovered.

As people begin to learn more about themselves by cultivating flexibility, and discover more about their interlocutors through curiosity, a new challenge may emerge: How exactly to respond? In other words: What should one do? What specific questions should be asked? Is this the right person to talk to? Am I going to be able to remain curious with *this* person? Should I invite her to something more? Should I walk away? Determining *how* to respond to an encounter in a polarized world can be the difference between the exchange of grace, or something less appealing. To move the exchange in the direction of a salvific moment, 'prudence' becomes necessary. I now address this important virtue.

Prudence in the Storm

Prudence is practical wisdom.[61] It involves making decisions in a given situation so as to bring about the greatest

---

60. For more on these types of questions, see Lee, *Talking Across*, 53–54. See, also, Kathy Taberner and Kirsten Taberner Siggins, *The Power of Curiosity: How to Have Real Conversations That Create Collaboration, Innovation and Understanding* (New York: Morgan James, 2015), 53–72.

61. See Robert Hariman, *Prudence: Classical Virtue, Postmodern Practice* (University Park: The Pennsylvania State University Press, 2003), especially at vii.

good for all those affected by the decisions. To act prudently requires knowledge of oneself, knowledge of the situation and people to which one is encountering, and insight into what might be the best decision to bring about the most favorable outcome for all involved.

For Christians (and others), being prudent requires a consideration of the needs and desires of the various people affected by any given decision or action. However, perhaps more importantly, prudence requires insight into God's will.[62] The prudent Christian prays to live and instantiate the words: "Thy will be done on earth as it is in heaven" (cf. Mt. 6:10). Ultimately, then, the prudent person seeks to discern God's will so as to make the best decisions to bring his will to fruition.

This is no easy task, to be sure. There is no guarantee that one can have full, or even partial, access to God's will, especially in particular situations. One's well-formed conscience, the Biblical witness, the Christian tradition, and the teachers of the tradition, provide a framework for understanding God's will. While it is important to remember that God's will is, in some respects, mysterious, God does desire to guide human beings that they might carry out the task of making God's will present on earth as it is in heaven—otherwise, Jesus would not have asked his followers to pray this particular way. What is needed, therefore, in order to be prudent, is a robust life of prayer where people open themselves up to the guidance and gift of God's direction.

To investigate how prayer and the gift of God's guidance can form prudent decisions that can bring about salvific encounters, I visit, one last time, the life and ministry of Jesus.

---

62. See Catholic Church, *Catechism*, nos. 1806, 1810.

The Prudence of Jesus in His Ministry

As God's Son, Jesus constantly sought his Father's will in prayer, and was open to guidance from his Father through the Holy Spirit throughout his entire ministry, to navigate the many situations and people he encountered (Lk. 4:14).

The Gospels depict Jesus being guided by the Holy Spirit of God from the very beginning. The Spirit accomplished the mystery of the incarnation through Mary to bring about the conception of her savior (Lk. 1:35). Subsequently, the Spirit led Jesus into the desert when the long-awaited time arrived for him to begin his ministry (Mt. 4; cf. Lk. 4).

Later in his life, standing up in the synagogue before the community, Jesus rightly appropriated and claimed for himself the words of the prophet Isaiah as he proclaimed: "The Spirit of the Lord is upon me, because he has anointed me to bring glad tidings to the poor. He has sent me to proclaim liberty to captives and recovery of sight to the blind, to let the oppressed go free, and to proclaim a year acceptable to the Lord" (Lk. 4:18-19). Christ could make prudential decisions in his ministry of crossing over and encountering the poor, the blind, the prisoner, and others—and responding to their many needs—because the Spirit was upon him and had anointed him.

There were other significant moments in the life of Jesus where it was evident that he was discerning his Father's will and remaining open to the guidance of the Spirit.

Take, for instance, when Jesus called his first disciples. This was no unimportant moment for the history of salvation. These people would become the foundation upon which the Church was built, and those sent to the nations to preach the good news.

Luke's Gospel says that: "In those days [Jesus] departed to the mountain to pray, and he spent the night in prayer to God. When day came, he called his disciples to himself" (6:12). He spent the *entire night* in prayer, seeking the will of his Father—begging his Father for guidance—so that he might act prudently in the world, and lay the foundation for his Church.

Another poignant example of Jesus' pattern of seeking his Father's will occurred just before he crossed into the 'storms' in Jerusalem. Retreating to the Mount of Olives, Jesus knew the *kairotic* time had arrived. He understood that he would be tested, tried, rejected, and beaten. He knew that great suffering was waiting for him. So that he might make prudential decisions along the way—knowing what to say and when, how to act, how to read and understand his interlocutors, and how to bring about the salvation of the world—he set himself to prayer.

The Gospel of Mark aptly depicts this special moment: "[Jesus] advanced a little and fell to the ground and prayed that if it were possible, the hour might pass by him; he said, 'Abba, Father, all things are possible to you. Take this cup away from me, but not what I will but what you will'" (14:35-36). Jesus prayed so fervently in this moment that Luke depicts him sweating "drops of blood" (22:44).

In this episode of great discernment and prayer, Jesus demonstrated to his followers what is required for those who desire to be prudent amid the storms of life. They must fall on their knees, seek to put aside their own will—their own expectations, desires, and agenda—and, in prayer and supplication, beg that God's will come to them, and be fulfilled in their life.

Seeking the guidance of God and God's will is an essential step in navigating a polarized world in a prudent way so as to bring about salvific moments. Of course—and this should be repeated—one cannot always know with certainty God's will in a particular instance. Because of this, those who seek to know and bring about God's will must always proceed in humility, lest they act imprudently, imposing their will on those around them, and impeding God's work of salvation in their lives.

This being said, there are practical items to consider when seeking to bring about salvific encounters in a prudent way. As we shall see, research on polarization is helpful in this regard. I now share some of this research.

The Importance of Prudence Based on the Science of Polarization

Alan Jacobs, in his book *How to Think*, provides practical wisdom to those who desire to engage in conversations with people who hold different views than one's own. According to Jacobs, when crossing over to engage the out-group other, people should seek out the best representatives of that group, "the smartest, most sensible, most fair-minded—representatives of the positions you disagree with."[63] Those who desire salvific encounters do not need to have conversations with everyone from the out-group—some people they encounter will simply not be disposed to facilitate meaningful conversations that assist both parties in growing in wisdom. Some people will be hostile; others will be uninformed. Not every interlocutor will share the love of wisdom, nor desire to pursue the truth of today's complex issues. The key, according to Jacobs, is to navigate the storm until one can find the most fitting interlocutor.[64]

---

63. Jacobs, *How to Think*, 75.
64. Jacobs, *How to Think*, 71–88.

Peter Coleman and his colleagues at the Difficult Conversations Lab offer two poignant pieces of advice that complement Jacobs'. First, Coleman recommends that people seek out pre-existing groups that can support them in their efforts of crossing over.[65] Not everyone will have the ability to approach the out-group other, engage them in conversation, remain curious, make prudent decisions during the exchange, *and do so alone*. A group of like-minded people who share the conviction about crossing over can provide support and strength. Many groups already exist that facilitate a rhythm of crossing over. Some of these will be explored in the following chapter.

Coleman also suggests that people need to remain patient as they seek to cross over.[66] Given that polarization in the United States has become exceedingly toxic, and that many of the issues that divide Americans have become intractable, people should not expect that one or two attempts at engagement will immediately improve the situation. In cases where divisions are entrenched, time is required for building mutual respect and trust between interlocutors, and for gathering information about the complex causes influencing disagreements. The effectiveness of crossing over for overcoming bias and deepening understanding is, as has been mentioned, confirmed in much research. Yet, depending on the severity of the divisions and the level of animosity that exists, time is often required before positive results are witnessed.[67] People should stay committed to the task at hand, persist in vari-

---

65. See Coleman, *The Way Out*, 210.
66. One of the crucial conclusions of Coleman's research is that overcoming certain intractable divisions requires much time. See *The Way Out*, 74–75.
67. See Coleman, *The Way Out*, 65–67.

ous moments of crossing over, and allow the passage of time as hearts begin to change.[68]

Cultivating Prudence

Given that prudence is necessary for bringing about salvific encounters, are there ways to cultivate this virtue? Much has been written on the cultivation of prudence, especially in moral philosophy.[69] For my purposes here, I offer two considerations; one is based on Christian wisdom, and the other on the science of polarization.[70]

First, to cultivate prudence, Christians will need to remain connected to the source of faith and of all practical wisdom, Jesus Christ. They will also need to embrace other members of the Christian community, and the assistance provided by the Church that Christ founded. For many people, this will include regular worship, partaking in the Sacraments of the Church, much time spent in prayer, and even the possibility of utilizing spiritual direction, so that people can process their experiences in the storms of polarization. Even though crossing over is essential to a person's identity in Christ, and as such should not be neglected, actively pursuing this way of life likely will mean becoming disorientated, frustrated, or confused. Therefore, Christians should not be naïve to think that they can maintain this essential aspect of missionary discipleship without regularly being fed themselves—fed

---

68. Coleman, *The Way Out*, 79.
69. See, for instance, Richard J. Regan, ed., *Aquinas: The Cardinal Virtues: Prudence, Justice, Fortitude, and Temperance* (Indianapolis: Hackett Publishing Company, Inc., 2005), especially chapter one.
70. For another source of prudential considerations for those dealing with polarization, see Amy Uelmen, *Five Steps to Positive Political Dialogue: Insights and Examples* (Hyde Park: New City Press, 2014).

by the sacraments, by prayer, and by communion with other Christians.

Second—and this is an important reality check—it might be the case that no one is really ever *fully* prepared to cross over. Everyone, including the most prudent, curious, and flexible people, will encounter challenges along the way. They will likely fail in many of their attempts to engage the other.[71] The possibility of failure, or the anxiety about not being prepared in the storms of polarization, can deter people from beginning this important task, especially for those who are most likely going to bring kindness, civility, and charity to moments of crossing over.[72]

Those writing on polarization encourage people to put aside these concerns and, if they are able, to act.[73] One of the best ways to grow in practical wisdom for crossing over is, ultimately, *to cross over*. Even if the experience of engaging the out-group other does not go as planned, prudence can come about from learning from one's experiences, reflecting on what went well, making adjustments according to what was learned, and trying again.[74] Important actions in life are worth attempting, and attempting again, even after failure.

Conclusion

Having provided some of the tools that can assist people in navigating the storms of polarization, it is important

---

71. On this point, see Coleman, *The Way Out*, 195–198.
72. See Bail, *Breaking the Social Media*, 68–83. See, also, Holland and Silvers, *I Think You're Wrong*, 1–19.
73. Holland and Silvers, *I Think You're Wrong*, 1–19. See, also, Coleman, *The Way Out*, 79; 184; 217.
74. Hariman, *Prudence*, viii.

to explore many wonderful examples of people who have utilized these tools and chosen to cross over. Doing so can be inspirational and heartening and provide a source of motivation to follow Jesus into the storms of life. It is these people and their examples that will be taken up in the final chapter of this book.

Chapter Seven

Hope in the Storm

Stories of Great Heroism

Hurricane Florence shifted south. For days, the storm was projected to move directly over the town where I lived. We were doomed. Then the path changed, and, just like that, we were spared.

Despite the altered trajectory, Florence's landfall was still memorable. Our town witnessed the spin-off of at least one tornado. Rain soaked the ground. Rivers filled. And winds managed to disrupt power. But the worst of the storm missed us.

When the weather system finally moved west and the rain stopped, people emerged from their homes and shelters. Driving around, I surveyed the minimal damage, and stopped to talk to those doing the same.

The stories from neighbors were similar. They had hunkered down, waited, recognized that the brunt of the storm would miss us, and were relieved when it was over. Many, sighing with gratitude, recounted how the town had suffered two hurricane-influenced massive floods in less than a few years. They did not think their town could take another hit. I imagine they were right. We were all grateful.

Then word reached us from Wilmington and other towns south of our location. Immense damage was reported.[1] Flooding. Even deaths. The storm went directly over them. It was going to take months, maybe years, to rebuild.

But the narrative from the residents of Wilmington and the surrounding areas was not overwhelmed by sadness and despair. Stories surfaced of great heroism. Families had sheltered the homeless in safety. Neighbors shared supplies. People used boats to rescue loved ones. Strangers were sacrificing to care for those who had lost nearly everything.

Though real and devastating, the destruction and sadness were, thankfully, eclipsed by displays of generosity, courage, sacrifice, and even love, in the face of the storm. These examples inspired hope, and, for those who were trying to put their life back together, encouraged them to persevere.

Unlike Hurricane Florence, the storms of polarization hovering over the United States are, sadly, not likely to pass anytime soon. As has been explored throughout this book, these slow moving, persistent, and intense systems have divided families, broken friendships, exposed and widened cracks in deteriorating political institutions, and fractured churches.

Yet, there are reasons for hope.

Even as people survey the damage caused by polarization, stories of virtue have emerged. Brave souls have reached out to those who seemingly despise them, seeking solidarity. Others have crossed over to the out-group— standing next to their repugnant cultural other—pursuing a personal change of heart. Church communities have

---

1. Visit the following website for more information: https://www.weather.gov/ilm/HurricaneFlorence.

worked through disagreements, recognizing the importance of their shared baptismal identity. Charitable dialogues continue throughout the United States on both the ecclesial and political level. Courageous conversations have elicited wisdom and deepened nuance. Jesus' incarnational movement has been extended, as salvific encounters have become reality.

In this final chapter, I want to leave readers with reasons for hope. Division, animosity, and rancor do not have to be all that remains in the wake of the hurricanes of polarization. In fact, they are not. Many stories and examples exist of people who, and organizations that, have taken up the challenge of crossing over, of seeking to overcome some of the negative consequences of polarization, and of attempting to bring about salvific moments in a polarized world. Harmonizing with the examples of the saints explored throughout this book, these contemporary people and organizations are witnesses, in their own way, to the Christocentric imperative of crossing over. Their stories deserve the final say.

Courageous Individuals in the Storm

Daryl Davis

It is fitting to begin a conversation about courageous individuals crossing over into the storms of polarization with the example of a remarkable man named Daryl Davis.[2]

---

2. For more on Daryl Davis, see Grant, *Think Again*, 121–141. See, also, Conor Friedersdorf, "The Audacity of Talking About Race With the Ku Klux Klan," *The Atlantic*, March 27, 2015, https://www.theatlantic.com/politics/archive/2015/03/the-audacity-of-talking-about-race-with-the-klu-klux-klan/388733/. See, also, Nicholas Kristof, "'How Can You Hate Me When You Don't Even Know Me?'" *The New*

Davis is Black. As a child, he admits he knew little about racism or prejudice. That all changed when, at the age of ten, walking in a parade with his mostly white Cub Scout group, he was singled out by spectators who threw objects at him.[3] This outlandish behavior required his fellow Scouts to circle around him to offer protection. Davis was confused. Why did they single him out? His parents later explained that the reason for the ill treatment was the color of his skin.

This traumatic moment left Daryl with a question about the human condition that would remain with him, and inspire him to be an agent working to undo division and racism: "How can you hate me when you don't even know me?"

Fast forward to Davis' adult years. He's now a professional musician. After finishing a performance in a bar in Maryland, a white man approaches, and, impressed, comments on his musical abilities. They begin to talk. Talking turns to sharing a drink. Little does Davis know that the man next to him has *never* shared a drink with a Black man. There's a reason for this. The white man is a high-ranking member of the Ku Klux Klan—a truth that would drop, much to Daryl's surprise, as they were conversing.

This small encounter in a bar between two unlikely interlocutors would result in friendship—and much more.

York Times, June 26, 2021, https://www.nytimes.com/2021/06/26/opinion/racism-politics-daryl-davis.html. See, also, Dwane Brown, "How One Man Convinced 200 Ku Klux Klan Members To Give Up Their Robes," NPR, https://www.npr.org/2017/08/20/544861933/how-one-man-convinced-200-ku-klux-klan-members-to-give-up-their-robes.

3. See Morena Duwe, "Daryl Davis: The Black Musician Who Converts Ku Klux Klan Members," *The Guardian*, March 18, 2020, https://www.theguardian.com/music/2020/mar/18/daryl-davis-black-musician-who-converts-ku-klux-klan-members.

After many long conversations about race and bigotry, the Klansman would ultimately choose to leave the Klan for good. The Black man would find his life's passion.

From that day, for nearly 40 years, Davis has befriended hundreds of Klansmen. He's attended their rallies, seen them burn crosses, listened to their hatred, and put himself in danger—real danger. Yet, many Klansmen—more than 200—on account of Daryl's bravery in the storm, have come to recognize the error of their ways and changed their life, leaving the Klan forever.

When asked about how he approaches this challenging task, Davis commented: "I would find things in common. And as I began to build on those commonalities, the things that we had in contrast—as trivial as skin color—begin to matter less and less. And as I built upon those commonalities a relationship was formed."[4] Stemming from his extensive experience, he provides an invitation worthy of note: "Take the time to sit down and talk with your adversaries. You will learn something, and they will learn something from you."[5]

Brother Craig Digmann, G.H.M.

Brother Craig's background and story are quite different than Daryl's, yet the pattern of crossing over and engaging the 'other' is similar.

Digmann, a white, middle aged man, is a religious brother in a missionary organization called the Glenmary

4. See "African-American Man Convinces Klansmen to Leave the KKK Through Friendship," *Fox 11 Los Angeles*, https://www.youtube.com/watch?v=PVVFx3issHg&t=98s.
5. Daryl Davis, "Why I, as a Black Man, Attend KKK Rallies," *TEDx Talks*, https://www.youtube.com/watch?v=ORp3q1Oaezw.

Home Missioners. As a Catholic serving in rural, southern counties in the United States, he's accustomed to living around the majority Protestant—mostly evangelical and Pentecostal—Christian population. He's also aware of the division that exists between Catholics and Protestants, where both sides often share the blame. This division is regularly coupled with misunderstanding, prejudice, and sometimes, even hatred.

Brother Craig feels inspired to overcome these divides.[6] He orders his life and mission around Jesus' prayer that all Christians would be one (cf. John 17). That members of the same Body of Christ could find reasons to hate each other is, to him, unacceptable, though he understands well the long, sad history of division between Christians. So, he devotes himself, one relationship at a time, to overcoming this hatred and bringing about unity. As he is known to say: "It's about relationships."

To build these relationships, he dedicates himself to visiting every church in the county in which he lives. This process begins by meticulously mapping out the churches, often hundreds of them, recording their address, logging contacts, and planning for a visit. Once mapped out, Brother Craig resolutely determines to fulfill his passion: to visit them all.

Arriving early at the various churches, Brother Craig often sees a few friendly faces he has met throughout the town—some have invited him to attend their services. With those he meets for the first time, he smiles, shakes hands, talks about the weather, comments on local high school sports, asks questions, and then readies himself to pray.

---

6. John Stegeman, "1 Body in Christ: Glenmary's 78-year History Making Mark on 500-year Rift," *Glenmary Challenge* (August 2017): 11–14.

He's aware that for many of the people he meets, he is the first Catholic that they have ever talked to.

Once the worship service begins, Brother Craig follows the lead of the congregation. As a Catholic who deeply loves the Mass, what he encounters is not his usual style of worship. The hymns are different, the sermons are usually longer, and some of the communities still practice 'snake-handling.' But Digmann bows his head, listens attentively, and sings (though he avoids the snakes).

In some situations, Brother Craig is called upon to lead a prayer in front of the group. This invitation to pray publicly in front of the congregation is remarkable in that he's often the first Catholic to cross the threshold of these worship spaces. Craig's presence in leading the prayer, along with the community's hospitality extended to him, image an important reality: that unity can exist even when there are differences.

Brother Craig's approach is humble and nonthreatening. As he states: "I have tried to not be intrusive or to force my faith on any I have met, but to walk with people wherever they are in their lives."[7] He's adamant about allowing the Spirit of God to guide him in making prudent decisions and adapting to the many situations he encounters. In his own working theology of mission, he states: "I often remind myself that the 'Spirit' is always with me, the Spirit is in control, and the Spirit 'knows' what it's doing. I just need to have an 'openness' to allow the Spirit to somehow work 'through' me."[8]

---

7. Cindy Taylor, "Brother Craig to Leave Union Mission," *Union County Shopper News*, May 25, 2016.

8. This is an unpublished theological reflection by Craig Digmann titled "Sharing Our Catholic Faith with Non-Catholics," November 2017.

In one of his assignments as a missioner, he visited nearly 200 Protestant churches. From these momentous efforts, it is easy to understand how Protestants in the area have considered him, a Catholic, their 'pastor.' Furthermore, those he encountered regularly sought his advice in church matters, asked him for prayers, invited him to talk about Catholicism, accompanied him to Catholic worship, and even called upon him to give the sermon in the absence of their own minister.

One Protestant man from the county where Brother Craig served summarized Digmann's presence like this: "[In] my numerous experiences of fellowship with him, [he] has exemplified a deep respect of my community and its culture. He has become one of us, exhibiting utmost kindness." The man continued: "We enjoy his presence in our community and his willingness to know our culture, our names, and even our struggles."[9] Few more complimentary words could be said about a person who has given his life to a mission of crossing over.

Chris Arnade

Race and religion, sadly, can be sources of division in American culture. Another potential dividing line is class, particularly between those who have so-called succeeded in society, and those who are struggling to do so.[10] Documenter and photographer Chris Arnade has dedicated himself to understand, and to stand in solidarity

9. This quote can be found in an unpublished survey Brother Craig conducted to learn more about how people were receiving his ministry of presence.
10. On the reality of class divide in American culture, see Isenberg, *White Trash.*

with, those who are often rejected and forgotten in main-stream culture—what he calls 'back row' America, referring to those who sat in the back of classrooms growing up, did not necessarily succeed academically in life, remained in their hometown despite little opportunity, and often found themselves on the streets, struggling with addiction.[11]

Arnade's story is unique. He has a Ph.D. in theoretical physics and worked many years on Wall Street, making, as he states, "a very good living."[12] During those years in the financial sector, he recalls being told by his colleagues, friends, and family, to avoid certain areas of New York City, particularly in the Bronx. Their perception was that those places were drug-infested, dangerous, and impoverished. He was warned not to visit them.

What did Arnade do? Curious, and unsatisfied with his work on Wall Street, he decided to cross over to those areas of New York City—and beyond—that most people wanted to avoid. From forgotten counties in rural America, to impoverished cities, Arnade decided to journey across the United States to meet, talk to, learn from, and hear the stories of, the people living in these areas. With him he took three things: a notebook to record the stories of the people he met, a camera to take photos, and a spirit open to learn. "I stayed in a town for as long as it took to force me to rethink what I believed,"[13] he comments.

Arnade discovered that one of the best ways to meet people was by spending time in the McDonald's fast-food restaurant in each place he visited. As he writes, "If you want

---

11. Arnade, Dignity, 45–47.
12. See Michel Martin, "Chris Arnade Spent Four Years Documenting 'Back Row America,'" *Amanpour and Company*, July 23, 2019, https://www.youtube.com/watch?v=p9asTn2HQ4w&t=773s.
13. See Martin, "Chris Arnade."

to understand the country, visit McDonald's."[14] Arnade recognizes that many people often judge McDonald's negatively for having unhealthy food or for paying low wages. However, in his opinion, for "the most marginalized—people who are living on the streets or addicts—McDonald's is extraordinarily welcoming, and it becomes a community center in many ways."[15] Most nights, when Arnade was traveling across America, he would record many notes and stories in his journal while sitting in McDonald's. This provided him moments to meet others, to listen to them, and to learn their story.

Other opportunities for meeting the people of the areas he visited occurred when locals approached him while he was walking on the streets. They would see him, walk up, and bluntly ask: "Why are you here?" He would simply respond: "I am here just to learn."[16]

He would then follow their lead. Some wanted to tell their story, others wanted their photo taken. Others were in need of assistance, which he sometimes provided. More than anything else, many of the people wanted to visit with someone who was willing to respect them and affirm their dignity.[17] As he states: "Most people didn't ask for money, even the most desperate. Most just wanted to sit and talk with someone who wasn't trying to save them, didn't scold them, and didn't judge them."[18] From prostitutes to addicts, Arnade sought to be this presence to many.

Beyond loving photography and being moved by the beauty of the areas and people he encounters in his visits,

---

14. See Arnade, *Dignity*, 37.
15. Martin, "Chris Arnade."
16. Martin, "Chris Arnade."
17. See Arnade, *Dignity*, 8.
18. *Dignity*, 16.

Arnade also desires to share what he has learned with others. He feels that the political structures of, and the decisions being made in, the United States, are not working for many Americans who are struggling to get by. He hopes his work can help others understand the plight of those who are often forgotten, and that his art can be a voice for those in need. Reflecting on his work, he states: "I wanted other people, in some senses, to see what I was seeing or to know what I was knowing, because I thought that the way our politics was aligned was not helpful."[19]

Much wisdom can be found in the many stories Arnade shares about the people he encounters in back row America. The photos in his book *Dignity* are priceless in their ability to capture the unique character of the areas of the United States he visited. Beyond those stories and pictures, he leaves people with this advice: "[Before] you judge somebody walk a mile in their shoes...When you see someone who is homeless or you see someone who is addicted or you see someone who votes the way you don't vote, before simply saying 'what a jerk' or 'what a lazy person' or 'they must have mental problems,' spend fifteen minutes talking to them and you will probably find out there is a lot more context to their story. And you realize the decision might be a little bit less crazy than you've realized."[20]

Hopeful Organizations in the Storm

In harmony with these and other examples of many courageous individuals responding to our polarized times are countless organizations seeking to facilitate moments

---

19. Martin, "Chris Arnade."
20. See Martin, "Chris Arnade."

of crossing over. Though I cannot cover them all here, mention of a few can provide further reason for hope in a polarized world, and likely stimulate creative responses.

Braver Angels

The 2016 election in the United States was, for many, a time of tension, division, and turmoil. Regardless of what outcome people desired in that election, many experienced deepening rifts caused by the polarizing tendencies of those months. People wondered: Is there any way to heal the country after what has taken place? No doubt, 2016 was not likely the first, nor will it likely be, unfortunately, the last time this question is uttered. However, for the people of Braver Angels, a nonprofit organization founded in the aftermath of 2016, there exists the belief that Americans from opposing political parties can find more in common than is often recognized, and that, even when differences and divisions exist, there can be mutual respect between fellow citizens.[21]

In the wake of 2016, the optimistic dreamers who would become the organizers of Braver Angels experienced what most thought was no longer possible. Outside of Cincinnati, Ohio, in the town of South Lebanon, the future founders of the organization brought together ten people who voted for Clinton and ten who voted for Trump. The purpose was simple: to see if these people, even despite what had taken place during the election, could speak to one another, learn from each other, and find common ground, along with mutual respect. The event was a success. From this moment a movement was born.

---

21. See https://braverangels.org/.

Braver Angels provides many resources and avenues to overcome negative polarization. It has, for instance, a podcast that seeks to include a diverse group of voices across the political landscape so that others may learn from the conversations. The organization offers online and in person training sessions to help people acquire skills to have difficult conversations with those with whom they disagree. Sources are also listed on its website to deepen people's familiarity with the contours and causes of polarization. What Braver Angels is most famous for, however, are 'red/blue' workshops—stemming from the creation moment in South Lebanon, Ohio, described above—that members continue to organize across the United States and online.

Imagine a convention room filled with a few dozen people. They are sitting together, conversing, and even laughing. From all indications, those gathered are enjoying themselves, and even forming friendships. And then, in an organized, public manner, conversations around political themes begin. People share, are heard, and participants respond to each other in a respectful way. The event goes so smoothly that it is hard to imagine that those participating in the red/blue workshop come from a variety of backgrounds, races, religions, generations, and, especially, political parties. Nevertheless, people are talking, sharing, and learning.

The purpose of these workshops is simple: "[To] bring Reds, Blues, and others together to talk, listen, and understand."[22] Remarkably—and the organization has conducted hundreds of events demonstrating this—people who cross over and enter into these workshops find that the stated goal comes to fruition. What is more, many

---

22. See https://braverangels.org/what-we-do/.

attendees walk away from the workshops inspired to learn more, hopeful about the future of the United States, and having acquired newfound friendships, many times with people from across the political divide.

What is in store for the future of Braver Angels? I had the opportunity to speak to co-founder David Lapp specifically about this question. Among other things, David is hopeful that the organization will increase its engagement within churches and faith communities. Though comprised of some members who are Christian, Braver Angels has primarily conducted its activities in civic and secular environments. Lapp believes, however, in addition to the work already being done by Braver Angels, that there is fertile ground to approach churches and ministers of all backgrounds to facilitate conversations around political issues that often cut through faith communities.

For instance, Lapp recounted that in early 2022, in the Archdiocese of Cincinnati, Braver Angels partnered with the Archdiocese, including members of diocesan staff. Together, they coordinated a red/blue workshop at a local parish, addressing specific political themes that are often the source of tension within Catholic, and other Christian, communities. Commenting on this new initiative, Lapp stated: "It's the same [red/blue] workshop but applying a Catholic lens to it."

During the workshop, Catholics had the opportunity to speak about the stereotypes they feel are directed toward them from fellow Catholics, articulate how those stereotypes do not accurately portray their experience of faith or politics, and highlight what is of value to them as Catholics who seek to take an active role in political life. This event with the Archdiocese was such a success, that Lapp hopes that Braver Angels could provide "a lot more help to parish pastors and dioceses to give them tools to address the political conflict that arises in parishes."

Throughout its short, though effective existence, Braver Angels has acquired wisdom and lived practices that can assist people in the storms of polarization. Much of this information can be found on their website. However, it is appropriate to close this section by referring to a quote that speaks to the heart of the organization. In the middle of the nineteenth century, when the United States was tearing in two, Abraham Lincoln (1809–1865) spoke profound words that, according to the founders of Braver Angels, are just as applicable today: "We [Americans] are not enemies, but friends. We must not be enemies. Though passion may have strained, it must not break our bonds of affection. The mystic chords of memory will yet swell the chorus of the Union, when again touched, as surely they will be, by the better angels of our nature."[23]

Divided We Fall

Throughout various sections of this book, I have indicated how media outlets and political pundits have an incentive to intensify the perceptions of the divisions that exist in the United States and to animate the negative feelings maintained both within, and directed outward toward other, political mega-groups. If American citizens and others only rely on network news outlets or social media to inform their political and cultural worldview, animosity and hatred toward the out-group other will likely only increase. In the face of this challenge, many organizations

---

23. See https://braverangels.org/our-story/#problem.

have emerged over the last decade seeking to overcome this problem. Divided We Fall is one of them.[24]

Promoting themselves as a nonprofit, online news outlet, Divided We Fall seeks to provide bipartisan dialogue for people interested in politics. In contradistinction to many news outlets that often only publish stories reinforcing a particular worldview or, worse, dehumanizing the out-group other, Divided We Fall is dedicated to publishing debates, interviews, and articles between individuals who disagree, so that various perspectives can be brought together and illuminated in one outlet. They seek to show that respectful engagement is not only possible, but beneficial, especially in polarized times.

In my conversation with Joe Schuman, founder and editor-in-chief of Divided We Fall, he described the purpose of the group as follows: "We launched the project about four years ago to try and give people that experience of informed opinion from both sides, so at least they can be exposed to different viewpoints." He continued: "Hopefully, they can also see what productive disagreement can look like, and, maybe in some cases, we can even start toning down the rhetoric and changing minds." More than anything else, he notes, "[Our] project is about popping bubbles and getting people exposed to different viewpoints."

Schuman's passion for cross-perspective engagement has been inspired by his own life journey, and his own recognition of living in a 'bubble.' Residing throughout his life primarily in 'blue-America,' during high school, college, and beyond, Joe has maintained contact with a family member who represents a different political perspective, and who has had diverging life-experiences than Joe. "He was my political pen pal growing up," he notes. "[When]

---

24. See https://dividedwefall.org/.

news would break, people would turn to this or that news station. I would usually email him...and say: 'Here's what I think about this; what do you think?'"

Schuman notes that though he and his relative have not necessarily convinced each other to change their perspectives, deep, mutual respect and admiration have been cultivated between them over the years. To the founder of Divided We Fall, shared respect and mutual understanding are vital in a polarized climate.

The organization's quite young and diverse group of advisors and contributors don't shy away from some of the most intense topics in American culture—race, guns, transgenderism, and abortion—to name a few. According to Schuman, they want to "lean into division, but do so in a productive and simple way."

To accomplish this, one approach they take is to seek out members of the elite class, who often drive the debate— sometimes in more polarizing directions—to address these potentially polarizing issues candidly. Their contributors are asked to respond thoughtfully and intentionally to an interlocutor from the out-group. Rather than speaking into the bubbles that exist, this engagement tends to 'pop' bubbles and expose people to various perspectives, and a renewed way of engagement.

In particular, Joe notes that writing a position piece expressly considering another's perspective, typically from across the aisle, often positively influences the one writing to think outside of partisan ideology, even as it helps broaden the horizons of those reading the article. And so that positions are fairly represented, the outlet's diverse group of advisors and volunteer staff painstakingly analyze the exchanges and push the conversation to greater and more robust nuance.

When asked about the fruit that has come from the organization's work over the last few years, and what gives him excitement when considering the future, Schuman notes that increased interest in bipartisan conversations and engagement has grown. He recognizes that there has been a grassroots movement of various groups like Divided We Fall, from Bridge Alliance to the Listen First Project, all dedicated to alleviating some of the negative polarization that exists in the American context.[25] "There are a few hundred of these [bridge-building] organizations that all have a different model and [reach a different] demographic." He is hopeful that these organizations will continue to collaborate and to communicate to further their mutually shared goals. He concludes: "[It] is cool to be part of this larger movement."

Sant'Egidio

As I have been describing in this book, in many situations, cultivating salvific encounters means, for Christians (and others), taking the initiative to cross over to engage someone, whether in person or online, who is on the margins or the peripheries of society, or to engage someone labeled as the out-group other—even a fellow member of the Body of Christ espousing different ecclesial or liturgical perspectives. Sometimes, however, the reverse is needed. What is required in order to cultivate salvific encounters is to allow the 'other' to cross over to you. In these cases, cultivating *hospitality* becomes essential for living in a polarized world, so that groups are prepared to welcome those who desire to cross over to them. Sant'Egidio, a Roman Catholic orga-

---

25. See https://www.bridgealliance.us/. See, also, https://www.listen-firstproject.org/.

nization of lay people committed to mission and peace, is a remarkable example of a community that seeks to uphold both forms of crossing over.

Founded in 1968, Sant'Egidio today has thousands of members across the world. Committed to praying together, reaching out to the poor, and standing in solidarity with those on the margins of society, members actively engage in the outward missionary movement of a life of discipleship. Some of these outward looking practices address specifically the challenges of inter-group conflict and division.

For instance, the community, through discernment and prayer, will choose to engage in areas throughout the world where conflict, violence, or divisions exist.[26] Encountering the people living in these turbulent spaces, members of Sant'Egidio will build relationships, what they call 'friendships,' with those on various sides of a disagreement or conflict.[27] As the group states regarding their approach to peacemaking: "Developing personal relationships and understanding the culture of the belligerent parties" are essential practices toward cultivating unity.[28] Having built 'friendships,' members of the Community begin to serve as a kind of bridge between divided groups,

---

26. See Austen Ivereigh, "Changing the World Via the Crucified: The Community of Sant'Egidio," *God Spy: Faith at the Edge*, December 22, 2005, https://oldarchive.godspy.com/reviews/Changing-the-World-Via-the-Crucified-The-Community-of-Sant-Egidio-by-Austen-Ivereigh.cfm.htm. See, also, Mario Giro, "The Community of Saint Egidio and Its Peace-Making Activities," *The International Spectator*, July-September, 1998, https://ciaotest.cc.columbia.edu/olj/iai/iai_98gim01.html.

27. See "Sant'Egidio's Method," *Sant'Egidio*, https://www.santegidio.org/pageID/30428/langID/en/SANT-EGIDIO-S-METHOD.html.

28. Ibid.

bringing together involved parties, in the hopes of fostering deeper unity.[29]

Another creative approach to crossing over by the organization can be seen in their willingness to contact isolated political leaders throughout the world who tend toward violence or the abuse of human rights.[30] Though seemingly contrary to normal diplomatic relations, this kind of ministry, made possible because Sant'Egidio is not associated with any political institution, has been shown to play a special role in cultivating peace in the world.[31]

Beyond these encouraging outward examples of crossing over, the community also seeks to cultivate a spirit of hospitality, so that others who find themselves embroiled in conflict may contact them. I had the opportunity to speak with Professor Andrea Bartoli, the President of Sant'Egidio's Foundation for Peace and Dialogue, who has been a member of the community for 52 years. He provided insight into the organization's special practice for building peace through hospitality.

Dr. Bartoli began by highlighting the outward missionary thrust of Sant'Egidio. He emphasized that, "a Church that is not missionary almost disappears." To further this work of the Church, he noted that, "Sant'Egidio is clearly outgoing in its own missionary work." "We reach out to people in search of salvific encounter that is for them and for us...We are participating with them in the salvation that comes from Christ."

---

29. See Roberto Morozzo Della Roca, ed., *Making Peace: The Role Played by the Community of Sant'Egidio in the International Arena*, trans. John Milsud (New York: New City Press, 2013). See, also, R. Scott Appleby, *The Ambivalence of the Sacred: Religion, Violence, and Reconciliation* (Lanham: Rowman and Littlefield, 2000).
30. On this theme, see Coleman, *The Way Out*, 99–100.
31. See Coleman, *The Way Out*, 100.

When it comes to cultivating peace in areas that are experiencing extreme forms of violence or division, Bartoli notes that, sometimes, it is necessary that leaders engaged in conflict take the initiative to contact Sant'Egidio. As he states, often, "the peace-work [of Sant'Egidio] is the reverse. It is the moment of hospitality, of making room." When a political leader desires to explore alternative, more peaceful ways to move forward—ways that can include decisions for peace—he can contact Sant'Egidio and begin a process of dialogue to explore what peace might look like in the given situation being encountered.

On the one hand, Sant'Egidio helps leaders deepen their own personal commitment to peace. As Bartoli states, "peace comes in the secret of the heart." What often is needed by leaders who contact the organization is the facilitation of a "process of conversion and self-correction—conversion and self-control" to understand that options other than war are available. Though Bartoli recognizes that only God changes hearts, Sant'Egidio can provide an avenue for grace to work in the hearts of leaders. They provide a process that helps to 'interrupt' the pattern of conflict that is often flowing from the decisions of leaders in uncertain situations.

On the other hand, Sant'Egidio, once receiving leaders who have crossed over to them, can explore, with those leaders, practical options for peace and justice. Given that the organization is now internationally known in the arena of peacemaking, they "make the options for peace more credible and more reasonable [for leaders who contact them]." "Clearly [there is an] interiority element [in the process of building peace]," says Bartoli, "but there is also a political one, which needs to be practical, which needs to be viable." He continues: "We encourage moves [decisions] which allow a person to be more of a peacemaker than they have been so far."

As I closed my conversation with Bartoli, I asked if Sant'Egidio has been contacted by groups in the United States, either by dioceses seeking to foster unity between polarizing factions in the Church, or by American government leaders, desiring to cultivate peace in conflicted cities or towns where racial discrimination or violence are prevalent. He mentioned that no one has contacted him yet with an offer to work in the United States on these issues, particularly around the challenge of polarization. He did, however, remain open to this possibility. "Maybe your book will serve as an invitation to consider these important themes," he said with a smile. "There is always a danger," he notes, "that the Church looks more like the world, becoming polarized, rather than the Church serving unity, the communion of the world." His desire is that Sant'Egidio, in their own small way, can help the Church foster the unity that Jesus desires for all people.

Creative Contributions in the Storm

Having explored courageous individuals and hopeful organizations facilitating a ministry of crossing over, I want to close this book by highlighting some examples of the kind of creativity that can accompany movements for unity. Efforts of crossing over do not have to be undertaken *only* by experts of conflict-management and peacebuilding, by church ministers or leaders, or by those readily committed to political action and involvement. Crossing over can flow from the talents, interests, and personalities of all people who have the desire to instantiate this important aspect of life in a polarized world—to imitate the witness of Jesus. Many examples exist of talents and interests being utilized in creative ways to contribute to salvific encounters in a polarized world. Here are just a few.

For instance, do you like to travel? For those interested in exploring new areas of the United States, Etgar36 provides a creative solution for overcoming some of the geographic sorting that can cause deepening polarization.[32] Their goal is to expose participants to areas and people of the United States that are somewhat foreign to them. Loading up buses and flying on planes, rural dwellers see cities, and urbanites experience rural communities. Included on the journey are debates, discussions, conversations, and meals with people representing various voices and backgrounds from across the United States, which provide participants the opportunity to see their fellow citizens in a new light.

Do you have a talent for cooking? Or, better yet, do you like eating tasty food? Justine Lee and Tria Chang, the organizers of Make America Dinner Again have discovered a creative way to bring together 'reds' and 'blues.'[33] Cook a good meal, prepare a nice table setting, and invite people from different out-groups to eat together, and participate in a civil dialogue about personal values and beliefs. Harkening back to the table ministry of Jesus, this attempt to bring together factions and unite them through sharing food continues to inspire many in the United States. In my own personal experience, similar methods of using meals to foster unity have functioned positively in church settings as well.

---

32. https://www.etgar.org/summer-journey/overview/.
33. http://www.makeamericadinneragain.com/index.html. See, also, Bethany Jean Clement, "With Make America Dinner Again, Politics Gets a Place at the Table," *The Seattle Times*, August 13, 2018, https://www.seattletimes.com/life/food-drink/with-make-america-dinner-again-politics-gets-a-place-at-the-table/.

Are you interested in learning more about your Christian faith or catechizing others, but are concerned that politics has warped your vision of Christianity? Glenmary member Father Steve Pawelk has hosted catechetical events in his mission parishes specifically focusing on polarizing themes that often divide parishes. How does he manage to navigate these contentious issues in a healthy way? People who desire to share their opinions in the group must begin their comments only by referring to either the *Catechism of the Catholic Church*, or the Bible. This process assists people in reorienting their thoughts and ideas regarding important theological, moral, or political questions around the foundations of the Christian tradition, and establishes those beliefs held in common by members of the same church who may come from different polarized factions. Not sure how to begin to hold one of these events? The United States Conference of Catholic Bishops, on its Civilize It webpage, has many resources that can stimulate creativity.[34]

Or perhaps you enjoy hearing from informed theologians, politicians, or public figures who are knowledgeable in political and theological themes, which require nuanced attention, especially in polarized times. The Georgetown Initiative on Catholic Social Thought and Public Life, led by Kim Daniels and John Carr, seeks to bring together in dialogue a diverse group of speakers to address some of the most important issues touching Americans in general, and Christians in particular. Their website advertises future

---

34. For a helpful set of resources, which can assist in guiding conversation around political and faith issues, see the USCCB's Civilize It page: https://www.usccb.org/civilizeit.

dialogues and provides access to many of the debates and conversations that have been held over the last few years.[35]

Maybe podcasts are your interest. I mentioned above the podcast offered by Braver Angels. Another option is that provided by Sarah Stewart Holland and Beth Silvers, authors of *I Think You're Wrong (But I'm Still Listening)*, a book which has been referenced in previous chapters. Together, they host the podcast Pantsuit Politics, where they tackle some of the most divisive issues plaguing the United States. Holland and Silvers come from different backgrounds and espouse diverse opinions, but they seek to model constructive engagement of difficult and potentially divisive issues.

Sant'Egidio was mentioned earlier as one example of a hopeful organization seeking unity. Other options exist, such as the Focolare Movement.[36] Founded in 1943 by Chiara Lubich (1920–2008)—a courageous woman thoroughly committed to living out Jesus' incarnational movement—Focolare is based on Christian principles of unity and dialogue, though the movement includes members from all types of religious and philosophical backgrounds. This group seeks to accomplish the great task of building bridges between various groups to deepen the realization of being one 'family of all people.'[37] The movement now exists in over 180 countries and over two million people share closely in its life and work. In the United States, the movement focuses specifically on the challenge of polarization, and attempts to provide the opportunities, along

---

35. For more information, visit: https://catholicsocialthought.georgetown.edu.

36. It is important to note that New City Press, the publishing house of this book, flows from the Focolare Movement.

37. For more on Focolare Movement, see https://www.focolare.org/en/.

with the skills, for people to alleviate some of the negative consequences of the current, contentious political and cultural milieu.[38] People who join this group will find other human beings who desire unity and are committed to the difficult task of crossing over, even despite the challenges existing in polarized times.

Conclusion

In many ways, the possibilities for crossing over and creating salvific encounters are endless. I've only begun to list above some of the many examples of hope in the storm. Wherever people of good will recognize the pains of polarization, are tired of the state of American political and ecclesial tensions, and desire to infuse the present negative milieu with grace, there are programs, people, and institutions seeking to provide a way out, to facilitate moments of crossing over, and to bring about the Kingdom of Unity, one salvific encounter at a time. I hope that this book has encouraged readers to continue to seek to do the same.

---

38. For an exploration of the Focolare Movement in the United States, see Thomas Masters and Amy Uelmen, *Focolare: Living a Spirituality of Unity in the United States* (Hyde Park: New City Press, 2011).

FOCOLARE MEDIA

Enkindling the Spirit of Unity

The New City Press book you are holding in your hands is one of the many resources produced by Focolare Media, which is a ministry of the Focolare Movement in North America. The Focolare is a worldwide community of people who feel called to bring about the realization of Jesus' prayer: "That all may be one" (see John 17:21).

Focolare Media wants to be your primary resource for connecting with people, ideas, and practices that build unity. Our mission is to provide content that empowers people to grow spiritually, improve relationships, engage in dialogue, and foster collaboration within the Church and throughout sociecy.

 Visit www.focolaremedia.com to learn more about all of New City Press's books, our award-winning magazine *Living City*, videos, podcasts, events and free resources.